THE GUIDE TO
BETTER ENGLISH

In this series:

English Dictionaries:

Workbooks – *Check your:*

Visit our website for full details of all our books: **www.petercollin.com**

THE GUIDE TO
BETTER ENGLISH

Philip Gooden

PETER COLLIN PUBLISHING

Second edition published 2001
by Peter Collin Publishing Ltd
32-34 Great Peter Street, London, SW1P 2DB

First published as *The Guiness Guide To Better English*, 1996
by Guiness Publishing

British Library Cataloguing-in-Publication Data

A catalogue record for this book is available from the British Library

ISBN 1-901659-66-6

Text computer typeset by PCP
Printed and bound in Finland by WS Bookwell
Cover artwork by Gary Weston

CONTENTS

Introduction

Good English. Correct English. The subject rouses strong feelings, with some. Others wonder what the fuss is about. Does it matter? Is the split infinitive a hanging offence or something perfectly acceptable? Are you sticking your neck out if you end a sentence with a preposition in a piece of writing? When is it all right (or OK) to use colloquial or slang expressions? Is it really significant if you pick the wrong word (confusing 'imminent' and 'eminent', for example) – people will generally know what you mean, won't they? This guide sets out to answer such questions. Unsurprisingly, the assumptions underlying this book are that good English exists and matters, that to take care over using the language is satisfying both for user and listener or reader, and that it's not so much a question of outright good or bad usage but of more (and less) effective ways in which we are able to express ourselves.

One can identify two distinct camps on opposing sides of the river of English. On the 'purist' bank are those who want to guard the language, to preserve it, and to put down irregular behaviour (nouns behaving as verbs, for example). These are the people frequently referred to in grammars and guides like this as 'some users' – a sizeable minority which is irritated or offended by slack and incorrect English. On the other bank of the river is the 'anything goes' battalion. Their argument runs roughly as follows: language is a living thing, shaped by users who, for the most part, pay little attention to the rules and practices of grammatical usage. The way in which the majority of users use the language is, almost by definition, the right way. The people on this bank rather enjoy thumbing their noses at the purists on the other side.

The 'anything goes' argument has a certain attraction. But it ignores the fact that English, like any other language, is governed by rules which <u>all</u> users observe whether they are aware of them or not. In English, as a 'rule', an adjective precedes the noun which it describes; as another 'rule' the verb tends to be placed in the early part of a sentence rather than at the end (except in questions). These are local customs. French and German follow the opposite practice with adjectives and verbs, respectively. All of us observe the basic rules of language. If we did not, choosing instead to speak and write our own version of English, with perhaps a random arrangement of words, an arbitrary choice of tenses, and so on, we would not be understood. No one would listen to us, no one could read us. Communication, the primary function of language, would break down. And, with English, communication is a more insistent and practical question than with almost any other language on earth. As a first language English is used by well over 300 million people; as a second language by almost a third of that number.

If the notion that good English can only be correct English is a little daunting, we can attempt another definition: good English, whether written or spoken, is language used with clarity, used effectively; a language that achieves the results a writer or speaker desires; and (where appropriate) a language deployed with polish and style.

Perhaps the most vital consideration in our use of English is the register we choose, the form of the language appropriate to a particular occasion. The register is revealing both about the speaker or writer and also about the intended audience. What, for example, do the following few sentences say, not so much in themselves but about the writers and their readers? What world-view do they encapsulate?

Others are expected to skive off on strike days...

Britain has 7 million old bangers still on the road.

Boozy Boris heart scare.

(all from the Sun)

Here is a world well supplied with 'skivers', 'old bangers' and 'boozers', a familiar place where plenty of people are on the make or the fiddle, driving dodgy motors and enjoying reading about the drinking habits of foreign heads of state. For the tabloid newspapers the world sometimes seems to be one big back garden, an impression reinforced by the cosy, slangy language and the relaxed phrasing. Such effects aren't confined to one corner of the press. A comment in the *Times Literary Supplement*, about a well-known author, read: 'Then he went ape, sending a letter of complaint to the paper.' Or an article in *The Times* talks about a well-known comic and his style: 'It leads straight into a rich seam of class disparity, in which the toffs can be snotty, the oik can be bolshie and everyone can get off on the sniff of danger.' The difference between these newspaper examples of colloquial and slang usage is perhaps that in tabloids like the *Sun* they are the staple while in the more upmarket papers they have an 'off-duty' feel. Whether formal, colloquial or slang, language is always revealing. Your choice of words and way of putting them together tells your listeners or readers (of letters, reports, memos, scribbled notes, anything) something about *you*, as well as about your attitude towards *them*.

As indicated above and in a number of the entries in the main section of this book (*see, for example,* Letter Writing *or* Slang) the style of everybody's speech and writing changes to suit the audience, whether it be one listener or reader or a thousand of them. This is obviously true of a carefully prepared and ceremonial event – the State Opening of Parliament, say – but it also applies to the seemingly most informal and robust occasions, such as a stand-up comedian entertaining a student audience. We have one voice for friends, most likely a different one for family, and almost certainly a further one for public consumption. This is to leave aside the specialist register we might employ at work or in some interest (falconry? surfing?) shared with a few other enthusiasts. Knowing how to use English effectively is very largely a matter of knowing which register to use and when to use it. Although there's something instinctive about this – most people learn very early on that there are things they hear at school and ways of saying those things which they wouldn't pass on to their parents – it is also a skill which is always in the process of refinement.

More than half a century ago George Orwell, the author of *1984* and *Animal Farm* formulated some 'rules' for good writing in an essay called 'Politics and the English Language'. Most are negative or prohibitive ('Never use a long word where a short one will do.'). Orwell's points are rigorous, even if he did not see them as unbreakable commandments: his final injunction tells us to break any of them 'rather than say anything outright barbarous'. Things have changed. We're not so happy with rules; at most we will accept 'rules'. What follows are a few suggestions, and more for written than for spoken English.

i) Think what you want to say before you start writing.

ii) The most impressive or effective writing is likely to be that in which the writer hasn't gone into contortions to show the reader how impressive and effective he (or she) is.

iii) Look at what you've written later, preferably after a cooling-off period so that you approach your own words in a more detached frame of mind.

iv) If you're not happy with something you've written it's likely your readers won't be either.

v) Break any and all rules once you know what they are.

Language is robust. English survives whatever we can throw at it – almost. English changes into, or stays, what the majority of its users wish it to be. But resilient as English is, it is not indestructible. Words get shapeless with misuse, they lose precision or they are combined in awkward, jarring formulations. A new use for an existing word may entail the disappearance of an older meaning. To fight a rearguard action against the misuse of, say, 'hopefully' or 'disinterested' could be called pedantic, but when the older meanings of such words have been buried under the newer definitions they will not be dug out again. English, like any developing language, is the accumulation of such gains and losses, and if gains are to be welcomed (sometimes), losses can also be prevented (occasionally).

The larger processes involving language and the changes in it are outside individual control, but language is a personal affair as well as the embodiment of some national sense of identity. How we say and write things is a reflection, a little blurred and distorted perhaps, of what or who we are. Saying and writing things well serves us well. We are understood better, and we can negotiate the world more effectively. Doing it well is enjoyable too. That is what this book is about.

Philip Gooden

Quotations in this book

Many of the examples of English, good, bad and indifferent, in this book are drawn from newspapers; some of the rest come from other types of writing, mostly fiction. Where I have not been able to find particular usages I have made up sentences to illustrate them. The newspapers most frequently cited are *The Times* *(www.thetimes.co.uk)*, the *Independent* *(www.independent.co.uk)* and the *Sun* *(www.thesun.co.uk)*, in all of which are to be found pieces which are vigorous or stylish, sometimes both together. Whether because the prose style in the broadsheets is more ambitious and complex than in the tabloids or because the broadsheets use more words or for some other reason, the prevalence of wrong or clumsy English is higher in the upmarket papers.

Marks used in this book

✗   A usage which is better avoided, i.e. a slight mistake

✗ ✗   A usage which should be avoided, i.e. a definite error

Entries in the main section of this book are arranged in alphabetical order. Where there is a cross-reference to another entry, this is indicated at the end of the entry, for example:
⇨ (See also ACRONYM, FULL STOP)

The definition of a word is underlined, and example sentences that show how the word has been used are printed in bold type.

ENGLISH – An alphabetical guide

A / AN

This is the aardvark of grammar books. The use of *a* or *an* is based not so
much on whether a word starts with a vowel or a consonant but on the <u>sound</u> of
the beginning of the word.

A is used before words beginning with a consonant sound:

a book, a tree, a United supporter

An is used before words beginning with a vowel sound:

an example, an octopus, an F. Scott Fitzgerald novel

H at the start of a word is generally sounded (house, helping) and sometimes
not (honorary, hour). *A* or *an* should be used accordingly:

a half but **an hour**; **a house** but **an honour**

With a few words the initial *h*, once unsounded, is now usually pronounced,
and therefore takes *a*. Some people continue to use *an* (as in *an hotel* or *an
historian*), but the habit is fading in writing. In spoken English, however, it can
persist, and this is one of those very rare instances in which the spoken word
lags behind the written:

'...described by the fire-chief as an horrendous journey.'

(quoted, Radio 4)

ABBREVIATIONS

There are thousands of abbreviations in circulation, from the very familiar to
the specialist. Abbreviations, whether of a single word (Mr, max. co.) or of a
group of words (mph, BT, CD), should be used only where the writer is certain
that readers will understand them.

Universal abbreviations, where the first letters of a group of words are used
much more often than the words are spelled out in full, rarely need explaining:
almost everyone knows what is meant by USA, BBC, AIDS, RSVP, NHS, TA,
plc, etc., even though few would be able to say what the abbreviations stand
for in every case.

When less common abbreviations are being presented to a wider audience,
for example in a newspaper, the convention is to spell them out in full first of
all:

...an extension of qualified majority voting (QMV)...

(Independent)

or to provide an explanation in brackets afterwards:

A researcher who rejects the ETH (extraterrestrial hypothesis)...

(The Times)

Terms which are well-known to a wide but still specialised audience may have to be explained when they occur in a more general context: for example, DTI and OECD would be easily recognised by the business reader but might have to spelled out in other contexts (Department of Trade and Industry; Organisation for Economic Co-operation and Development).

Care sometimes has to be taken over multi-purpose abbreviations: a leaflet advertising 'PC Awareness Training' turns out to be offering computer instruction rather than information about Political Correctness (let alone a Police Constable).

Full stops can be used to indicate abbreviations, but the tendency is to leave them out (AD rather than A.D.; UK, not U.K.) although they have a clearer function when they show that only the first syllable of a word appears and may occasionally prevent ambiguity (Sun.; Jan.1st; Chap. 7).

⇨ (See also ACRONYM, FULL STOP)

ACCEDE / EXCEED

The verb *accede* has two meanings: to <u>agree to</u> (with an overtone of 'surrender to'); and to <u>come into a position of state</u>:

We had no choice but to accede to their demands.

William III acceded to the throne after James II.

(The noun associated with this second sense is *accession*.)

To *exceed* (associated noun: *excess*) is to <u>go beyond</u> or to <u>outdo</u>; whether it is a term of praise or criticism depends on the context:

We'd heard the play was good but it exceeded our hopes.

ACCEPT / EXCEPT

Probably because of the tendency in standard English to pronounce the opening vowels similarly, the two words are occasionally confused as verbs, despite almost opposed meanings. To *accept* is to <u>receive</u>:

I accepted her kind offer of help.

The less common verb to *except* is to <u>take out</u>, to <u>exclude</u>:

He was excepted from the criticism which the rest of the committee earned.

(The related noun forms are *acceptance* and *exception*.)

ACRONYM

Like an abbreviation, an *acronym* is composed of the initial letters of a group of words:

AIDS	Acquired Immune Deficiency Syndrome
NASA	National Aeronautics and Space Administration
NATO	North Atlantic Treaty Organisation

| **QUANGO** | Quasi-autonomous non-governmental organisation |
| **UEFA** | Union of European Football Associations |

An *acronym* must be able to be pronounced as a word of one or more syllables. An abbreviation, on the other hand, remains a cluster of letters, each of which is pronounced separately (AA, BBC, rsvp).

Some collections of initials can be pronounced either as *acronyms* or spelled out by their initial letters:

UFO	yew-eff-oh, but treated as a word, not a set of initials, when making UFOlogy or UFOlogist
VAT	normally spelled out, unless attached to an inspector: VATman
NEDC	National Economic Development Council, which in the days when it mattered in British economic life was known, with affection or mockery, as 'Neddy'

Sometimes the cart is put before the horse and the words are chosen to make an appropriate *acronym*, rather than the acronym springing naturally and unforeseen from the initial letters. In the late 1960s Valerie Solanas founded SCUM (Society for Cutting Up Men); as good as her word, she later shot and almost killed the pop artist Andy Warhol.

⇨ (See also ABBREVIATION)

ACTIVE OR PASSIVE?

⇨ See VERB

ADJECTIVE

An *adjective* is a word added to a noun or associated with a pronoun and giving additional information about such things as colour, size, shape, age, and so on. Some of the stylistic and grammatical questions connected with adjectives are dealt with below.

HOW MANY?
Excessive use of adjectives is sometimes regarded as one of the marks of a clumsy or a novice writer, perhaps on the grounds that nouns ought to be allowed to speak for themselves without being smothered by a pile of subsidiary words. Listing <u>all</u> the attributes of a person or place, an object or a state of mind, may give the impression that the writer is being fussily precise, particularly where something simple is being described. A description of, say, a dining-table that listed all the terms that might be applied to it – <u>four-legged</u>, <u>oval</u>, <u>gleaming</u>, <u>mahogany</u>, <u>cared-for</u>... and <u>old</u> and <u>large</u> and <u>valuable</u>, among other things – would quickly exhaust a reader's patience. However, the writers cited in the next section (Gerald and Lawrence Durrell, and Iris Murdoch) are fond of piling up the adjectives, and have a reputation as stylists – so there are

good precedents for being open-handed with adjectives. As a general rule, though, it is worth applying the brakes after the first two or three adjectives, and asking yourself whether all that additional information is really necessary.

PUNCTUATION OF ADJECTIVES IN LIST

No comma should separate a single adjective from the noun which it precedes. A list of adjectives positioned in front of a noun may be separated by commas if they are of equal descriptive 'weight':

He had all the sleek, smug self-possession of a cat in season.

(Gerald Durrell, My Family and Other Animals)

"I had forgotten," he said, "what a civil, safe, friendly, decent, orderly little country England is."

(letter quoted in The Times article)

(no comma comes between 'orderly' and 'little' in this example because 'little country' is being treated almost as a compound noun.)

Although the tendency is to include commas between adjectives in front of a noun they can be omitted:

His walk is the slow rolling grinding trudge of a saint walking on Galilee.

(Lawrence Durrell, Justine)

However, an adjectival list that follows a noun or pronoun must be separated by commas. In the following example the commas are left out in the first sentence where the adjectives come in front of the noun *faun*, but included in the second where the adjectives come after the pronoun *he*:

He had been a slim tripping blond-haloed faun. Now he looked coarse, fat, red-faced, pathetic, slightly wild, slightly sinister, perhaps a little mad.

(Iris Murdoch, The Black Prince)

COMPOUND ADJECTIVES

When two or more words form a single adjectival concept they should be linked by hyphens:

A woman was sent on a <u>120-mile</u> round trip by ambulance looking for an incubator for her <u>soon-to-be-born</u> baby.

(Daily Star)

...the glass-sided hearse drawn by six <u>black-plumed</u> horses, the black <u>top-hatted</u> undertakers, the <u>close-cropped</u>, <u>barrel-chested</u>, <u>iron-jawed</u> bodyguards in their dark suits...

(Guardian)

Hyphenation applies whether the adjectives are familiar (as **black-plumed,**

close-cropped) or freshly made for the occasion:

> ...the frequently <u>homesick-for-the-womb</u> and <u>sick-to-the-heart-of-touring</u> lyrics...
>
> *(The Times)*

Leaving out the hyphens may cause ambiguity. (There's some in the second example above: was it the undertakers or their top hats that were black? Or both?) The following is a hyphen-free zone:

> ✘ But as anyone who has been through marriage counselling can tell you, there is no such thing as a value free marriage counsellor... What happens now if you cannot come to a private agreement is that you find yourself right back in that dirty linen eating adversarial court.
>
> *(Maureen Freely, Guardian)*

(a free marriage counsellor or a value-free one? Well, it's obvious enough what the writer means, but the hyphen would have made it clear straightaway. And 'dirty-linen-eating' is presumably one big, chewy compound adjective.)

⇨ (See also HYPHEN)

COMPARATIVE & SUPERLATIVE

'Comparative' describes the adjectival form where similar or identical qualities possessed by two things are compared (bigger / smaller than).

The 'superlative' applies to the form of the adjective indicating that something is the best (or worst), tallest (or shortest), etc. At least three things must be in question if the superlative is to be used correctly.

Almost all adjectives can appear in the comparative and superlative form, either by adding '-er', '-est' to the end of the adjective or by putting 'more' or 'most' in front. As a rule of thumb, with adjectives of a single syllable '-er' and '-est' should be added:

> **high / higher / highest**
>
> **red / redder / reddest**

Two-syllable adjectives ending in '-y' form the comparative and superlative in the same way – **funny / funnier / funniest** – but most other adjectives of two syllables and all those of three syllables use the more / most formula:

> **hopeful / more hopeful / most hopeful**
>
> **dangerous / more dangerous / most dangerous**

A handful of the most common adjectives change form when they move into the comparative and superlative:

> **good / better / best**
>
> **bad / worse / worst**
>
> **much / more / most**

Use of the comparative should be restricted to a comparison between <u>two</u> things:

> **Mayall comes out as the better of the two actors by most critics'
> reckoning.**
>
> *(The Times)*

The superlative should be used when <u>three or more</u> people or things are
concerned:

> **the youngest of the three sisters; the most intelligent member of the
> class**

With the comparative and the superlative the comparison may be implicit, i.e. a
word like 'than' or a phrase like 'in comparison to' does not necessarily
appear:

> **He's my younger brother.**
>
> **Canary Wharf is the tallest building in Britain.**

It's quite usual to find the superlative form used when only two things are
being compared:

> **✗ When the path in the wood forked he chose the one that looked least
> travelled on.**

(should be 'less travelled on' as two things only are in question. Although the
superlative is often used in speech and informal writing when the comparative
would be correct, careful usage requires the distinction to be made between
references to two things and to three or more.)

ABSOLUTE ADJECTIVES

A handful of adjectives describe an absolute state, one which cannot be added
to or taken away from, and these words should not, correctly speaking, be used
in the comparative or superlative form: examples include **complete**; **extreme**;
unique; **empty**; **full**; **total**; **absolute.**

In practice, we talk about *more extreme* and *emptiest*, though not *more total*
or *absolutest*. General usage is the best guide here; what sounds right to the ear
is likely to be all right on paper. However, a careful writer – at least in formal
contexts – would avoid *more complete* or *fuller*.

⇨ (See also NICE, UNIQUE)

ADVERB

An *adverb* qualifie: a verb, giving information about how an action is
performed. Adverbs are also used to qualify adjectives.

POSITION OF ADVERB

Different placings of the adverb within a sentence can change the meaning of
that sentence, and accordingly the adverb should go as near as possible to the
word (verb, adjective) with which it is associated:

> **He rejected their totally inflexible approach.**

He totally rejected their inflexible approach.

(In the first sentence *totally* tells us about their approach and its inflexibility; in the second, *totally* characterises his rejection.)

Sometimes the adverb may be removed altogether from what it qualifies and placed at the end of the sentence for emphasis:

He rejected their inflexible approach totally.

but this word order is more often found in spoken than in written English.

⇨ (See also ONLY)

'THE LAD DONE GOOD'

The colloquial use of the adjectival form of a word when by the rules of grammar an adverb form is demanded – as in the American 'I'll be with you real quick' or in the very English 'The boy done good in his first match.' – is not acceptable in written English.

TORTURED ADVERBS

Most adjectives can be transformed into adverbs by the addition of -ly, although the usual considerations of harmonious sound and familiarity should apply. These made-up adverbs sound all right:

...this, yet another first film, is jaw-droppingly, eye-bogglingly awful.

(Guardian)

But the following would have sounded better if 'ongoing' hadn't been forced to do a job it was unequipped for:

'All our tradesmen are thoroughly vetted and ongoingly monitored.'

(AA spokeswoman quoted on Radio 4)

Similarly for this made-up adverb:

"You aren't clear-cuttedly Europhile or Europhobe?"

(interviewer on Channel 4 News)

⇨ (See under HYPHEN for compound adverbs)

ADVERSE / AVERSE

The adjective *adverse* means <u>opposing</u> or <u>unfavourable</u>:

Adverse weather conditions delayed the crossing.

Averse means <u>reluctant about</u>, <u>unwilling</u>, and generally describes people's responses:

He was averse to the upheaval involved in the move.

Averse is usually coupled with 'not' – as in 'I'm not averse to your suggestion.' Although the phrase is sometimes objected to as a faintly pretentious understatement it indicates a willingness to be persuaded rather than enthusiasm about something, and therefore carries a valuable shade of meaning.

(The associated nouns for *adverse* are *adversity*, meaning <u>misfortune</u>, <u>hostile circumstances</u>; and *adversary*, meaning <u>opponent</u>. The noun associated with *averse* is *aversion*.)

ADVICE / ADVISE

Advice is the noun form, *advise* the verb:

We received some good advi̲ce / He advi̲sed us well.

(But the person giving the *advice* is an *advi̲ser.)*

The pronunciation differs according to whether one is using the noun or the verb. The change from the 'c' sound in the noun (*advice*) to the 's' in the verb (*advise*) is a guide to the changes in a number of other words which switch between 's' and 'c' spellings. In all cases they conform to the *advice/advise* pattern.

⇨ *See also* DEVICE / DEVISE; LICENCE / LICENSE; PRACTICE / PRACTISE; PROPHESY / PROPHECY

AFFECT / EFFECT

This is a very frequent confusion. As a verb *affect* means <u>to have an impact on</u>, <u>make a difference to</u>:

Peter's drinking affected his health more than his personality.

Harry Enfield, *Independent on Sunday*

To effect is <u>to bring about</u>, <u>to carry through</u>:

...Siouxsie & the Banshees have effected the most dramatic transformation..

The Times

In the following examples the writers have used *effect* when *affect* is required:

✘✘ **Concern about job security now effects everyone from mandarin to road sweeper.**

The Times

✘✘ **... competitors who can effect every participant's market share by their own price rises or poor performance.**

The Times

Confusion over this pair of words is almost inevitable. They sound nearly the same, and the noun which relates to the verb *affect* and has the same general sense of <u>impact</u> is not, as one might expect, *affect* as well but *effect*:

The harmful effects of cigarette smoking are now well established.

So the following are wrong:

✘✘ **And he had the same affect on his players.**

Sun

✗✗ ... the crash of 1929 still had profound affects on law and order.

Independent on Sunday

As a verb *affect* also has the meaning of to put on, to pretend:

Donovan wasn't ready to affect his Yorkshire accent at a press conference yesterday.

The Times

And as a noun *affect* (with the stress at the beginning: *affect*) has a psychological, specialist sense of emotion or desire. In this sense, it is not an everyday word.

The adjective *disaffected*, followed by 'with', means alienated from, not well disposed towards.

ALL RIGHT / ALRIGHT

The spelling *alright* is widely used, especially in informal contexts – **It'll be alright on the night** – but is regarded by some as less correct than *all right*, and is better avoided in formal writing. *Alright* is frequently a synonym for the more colloquial OK (**"Are you feeling alright?"**).

It is possible to see a distinction in meaning between the two spellings here:

He got the answers all right. (i.e. all correct)

He got the answers alright! (where the word functions as a strong affirmative exclamation)

ALLUSION / ILLUSION / DELUSION

Of these three nouns *allusion* has a meaning distinct from the other two. An *allusion* is an indirect reference:

The symphony made musical allusions to half a dozen works by other composers.

Illusion and *delusion* are both to do with a mistaken idea or a false belief. Of the two *illusion* is the more benign. Having *illusions* suggests ignorance but the experience may be a pleasant one – before they are, in any case, destroyed by harsh reality:

For a time the negotiators had the illusion that they would quickly achieve peace.

A *delusion*, however, is not something that is easily dispelled by argument or brutal fact; it may be a sign of madness:

He began to suffer from the delusion that he was Napoleon.

ALLUSIVE / ELUSIVE

Allusive is the adjective from *allusion*, and means hinting, referring in an indirect way:

He spoke with tact, treating the failings of his predecessor in allusive way, and not mentioning them explicitly.

Elusive means <u>hard to capture</u>:

The Loch Ness Monster has been a highly elusive quarry for researchers and hunters.

A LOT

Two words always – but it's not uncommon to find them written as one, probably because pronuciation runs them together:

✗✗...you will have alot of client contact.

(recruitment advert.)

ALTAR / ALTER

Altar (a noun) is the <u>communion table</u> in church or a <u>place for making sacrifices</u>.

Alter (verb) means to <u>change</u>.

ALTERNATE / ALTERNATIVE

Alternative can be used as a noun or adjective, and indicates that a choice is being offered. Originally the word was restricted to contexts where no more than two options were available, but it is often used now to indicate a wider range of choices. In this example, *alternative* is used with precision, because only two things are on offer:

Recently I've found the Open University programmes shown in the early morning...a far less stressful alternative [to breakfast television].

(TV science critic)

As an adjective, *alternate* means <u>occuring by turns</u>, <u>every other</u>:

We make deliveries in your area on alternate Thursdays.

The verb *alternate* means <u>to shift from one thing to another, and then back again</u>:

Her moods alternated between euphoria and gloom.

It is preferable to avoid using the adjectival form as a substitute for *alternative*, as here:

✗ Egyptologist Dr Daniel Jackson... walks through the stone portal into an alternate world ...

(Time Out)

✗ The city was an alternate target and was bombed two days earlier than planned.

(Guardian)

(This suggests that the city was bombed by turns with another target.)

Alternative also has wide currency as an adjectival term describing off-beat or unconventional technology, medicine, fashion, comedy, etc.

ALTOGETHER / ALL TOGETHER

Altogether (an adverb) means <u>entirely</u>, <u>with everything included</u>:

The couple were altogether delighted with their presents.

He made seven trips during the year altogether.

All together means occurring <u>simultaneously</u> or <u>in the same place</u>:

At the end of a traditional whodunit the suspects are summoned all together for the unmasking of the murderer.

AMBIGUOUS / AMBIVALENT

Ambiguous is an adjective meaning <u>unclear</u>, <u>of doubtful meaning</u>:

Astrologers usually couch their predictions in ambiguous terms.

Ambivalent means <u>being in two minds, experiencing conflicting emotions about something</u> (love / hate; attraction / revulsion).

Some people's attitudes to the National Lottery are ambivalent: glad that money is raised for good causes, unhappy at the 'culture of greed' which it seems to promote.

AMBIGUITY

Ambiguity in speech or writing is the failure to make one's meaning clear. The term is generally applied to a statement or action whose meaning could be understood in different ways – such as:

'We have to keep them.'

(comment about the Royal Family in a *Channel 4* documentary. Only the context made clear that what the speaker meant was not, 'We must hang on to the Royal Family', but more critically, 'We've got to pay for their upkeep.')

'Do you think the Prime Minister should go?'

(*Radio 4* interviewer, who quickly realised the ambiguity of what he'd said by adding – 'To the summit, that is.')

Ambiguity in speech can usually be cleared up on the spot, either because the speaker's tone makes the meaning clear or because he or she can generally be asked what was meant anyway. In writing the exact meaning may not always be so simple to determine. There is such a thing as 'creative' ambiguity, where the two possible meanings of a phrase are deliberately exploited:

The perfect mother's day present

(mobile phone advertisement)

(Which is perfect – present or mother? In adland it is both, of course.)

David Lodge is in a brown study...

(beginning of a *Guardian* article which went on to mention the khaki and beige furnishings of the writer's study. But the other sense of 'brown study' – thoughtfulness – was also relevant to the article.)

There is the often comic ambiguity which results from compressed or awkward phrasing:

Husky race protests

(*The Times* headline about Alaska dog-sled races and not an ethnic group with collective sore throat)

Dead fish wash up in Sydney

(*The Times* headline about pollution rather than after-dinner help in the Australian kitchen)

We have 100 copies to give away to lucky readers drawn from our postbag.

(Sun)

Real ambiguity is rare – that is, cases where the writer's meaning may genuinely be in doubt, if only briefly – but the writer should be alert to possible misreadings:

He was 90 years old when he kicked the bucket on the beach.

(This could be proof of his fitness, or, more likely, a metaphorical way of referring to his death.)

Blind people don't miss much.

(Matthew Parris, *The Times*)

(The rest of the paragraph showed that he meant that the other senses of blind people compensate to an extent for their disability. The sentence did not mean that blind people don't miss much because there's nothing much to see anyway.)

AMEND / EMEND

Both verbs have the sense of to <u>make better</u>. To *amend* is <u>to improve by correcting</u>:

Parliament amended the bill several times before it became law.

To *emend* has a more restricted sense: to <u>make alterations in a written text</u>:

He emended the proof copy before returning it to the printers.

The nouns from each verb are *amendment* and *emendation*.

AMERICANISMS

Americanisms are words and expressions which have crossed the Atlantic and embedded themselves in British English. Some, indeed, have spread further and gone round the world: **OK**; **gas station**; **Have a nice day**. Americanisms that give a name to something which previously had no name – usually because the thing in question came into existence only in the later part of the 20th century – are as useful and welcome as any new word that has to work for its living: **commuter**; **junk food**; **soap opera**. Other terms are in the process of pushing out their British cousins. **Apartment** has gone some way towards replacing the less glamorous-sounding **flat, elevator** is commonly used for **lift, gas** for **petrol**. The dynamism and universal spread of American culture explain this cuckoo-like tendency to dislodge native words from their nest. Some American usages are still alien to British ears even if they are widely understood: **Fall** for **autumn**, for example, or **diaper** for **nappy**, **windshield** for **windscreen**. And the use of an Americanism when the particular word hasn't yet achieved wide currency on this side of the Atlantic and when there is a pefectly good English alternative can suggest a rather strenuous desire to come across as modish. Certainly there are many English speakers who dislike Americanisms.

There is a small potential for confusion between American English and British English where a word means one thing there, another thing here. Some of the principal examples follow:

American	British
pants	trousers
vest	waistcoat
suspenders	braces
trunk	car boot
hood	bonnet
sidewalk	pavement
purse	handbag
band	ring
fall	autumn

AMERICAN SPELLING

A few words are spelled in different ways in US and British English. On the whole, American spelling better reflects the sound of the word: theater; center; humor; neighbor; check (for British English cheque); catalog.

A handful of American spellings are now commonly used in British English: e.g. encyclop(a)edia; medi(a)eval.

Several verbs which, in British English, can be spelled with '-ise' or '-ize' as a suffix take only '-ize' in American English: analyze; civilize; organize.

Another group of verbs ending '-al' in British English double the final letter in the infinitive / present tense in American English: appal(l); enthral(l); fulfil(l).

AMIABLE / AMICABLE

Both adjectives are to do with friendliness but have different applications. *Amiable* means <u>friendly</u>, <u>likeable</u>:

He was popular for his easy-going amiable manner.

Amicable means <u>in a friendly spirit</u>, and tends to be used in those contexts where differences of opinion have been resolved without a quarrel, or where bad relations might be expected:

After the divorce they made an amicable division of the property.

AMPERSAND

The ampersand (&) is used informally as a substitute for 'and', and is the standard way of linking two names in company titles:

Marks & Spencer

Crabtree & Evelyn

AT&T

It shouldn't be used in formal writing, and looks odd if it is combined with 'and' fully spelled out:

We provide top drawer senior Secretaries up & down the country and for companies abroad.

(recruitment advertisement)

AND and BUT AT START OF SENTENCE

There has long been an unofficial 'rule' that one should not start a sentence with *and* or *but*. Conjunctions, of which *and* and *but* are the most commonly found examples, are link words, so there is an element of logic in the belief that they should operate within a sentence and not at the start of one.

Nevertheless, the two words are often found at the beginnings of sentences, particularly in advertisements:

But don't worry, you won't find any commissioned salesmen...

And that's a promise.

(car / car hire advertisements)

There is no reason not to use *and* or *but* at the start of a sentence, although the writer should have some stylistic effect in mind when doing so. Putting *But* first stresses the word itself and also throws into relief the fact, opinion, etc. that follows, possibly because it is offered up in isolation rather than being part of a lengthier sentence.

Repeated use of *And* to start sentences can become an irritating mannerism. It's as if the writer is saying: Here's one thing. And here's another. And here's something I forgot to put in earlier. And so on.

However, using the conjunctions to start sentences is acceptable in good, reasonably formal written English and can be effective:

McThune did not take orders from any US Attorney, and at this moment he was sick of Roy Foltrigg. And the idea of using three or four overworked agents to follow an eleven-year-old kid was quite

stupid. But, it was not worth the fight.

(John Grisham, *The Client*)

⇨ (See also SENTENCE)

ANTICIPATE / EXPECT

These two verbs are widely treated as if they were interchangeable but there is a useful difference in meaning between them. *To anticipate* is not merely to believe that something will happen (i.e. *to expect*), but to take some action to prevent or lessen the consequences of what will occur. Where *expect* is largely passive:

They're expecting it to rain tomorrow.

anticipate has more active overtones:

[He] said the move was an attempt to anticipate the recommendations of the Greenbury inquiry ...

(The Times)

Anticipating a storm, the captain ordered the crew to batten down the hatches.

ANTI-CLIMAX

The impression produced by an *anti-climax* (sometimes known by the term bathos) in speaking or in writing is usually unintended. It is essentially a clumsy arrangement of material, so that some trivial or relatively unimportant point follows a series of impressive or significant ones.

Things were going from bad to worse, he claimed: society was breaking down, families were splitting up, violence was commonplace, unemployment was rising, and, to cap it all, the milkman no longer delivered.

The effect of such an *anti-climax* is always funny, whether the speaker / writer intends it to be or not. Anybody producing a list of points in an argument, or arranging events in a narrative so that the progress is from the lesser to the greater, needs to ensure that he or she is really ending on the thing that matters most, or is at least equal in importance to what's gone before.

APOSTROPHE

The apostrophe has two uses: to indicate possession and to show where letters have been left out of words.

POSSESSION:

This use probably causes more confusion than any other single piece of punctuation. Apostrophes are mistakenly tacked onto the end of ordinary plurals, and sometimes the third person singular of a verb, where they are never required. They are left out in places where they should be included. And

even when it is understood that an apostrophe is necessary there is frequent
uncertainty about its positioning (before or after the final s̲?).

APOSTROPHES WITH NOUNS
In the singular form of a noun the apostrophe is placed directly after the noun
and <u>before</u> the s̲, which is not here the sign of a plural but an indication of
possession (i.e., that the noun in some sense 'owns' the word which follows it):

a soldier's rifle
a day's work
a dog's tail
the earth's orbit

In the plural version of these words the apostrophe goes <u>after</u> the s̲, which is
already in place to signify the plural form of the noun rather than possession:

the soldiers' rifles
two days' work
the dogs' tails
(and if there were more than one earth)
the earths' orbits

In speech it's not always possible to tell whether a singular or plural sense of
the noun is intended (although the overall context of a remark will generally
make clear which it is that the speaker means). **My friend's cars**, for example,
could refer to one friend or several <u>as the listener hears it</u>. But written down it
can refer to one friend only. (Two or more would be **My friends' cars**.)

The exceptions to this rule – apostrophe before s̲ in the singular, after s̲ in
the plural – come with irregular plural forms, i.e. those nouns that don't simply
add s̲ when they are multiplied. Although a small minority in English, irregular
plurals are found with some of the most familiar words:

a child's toy and **children's rights**
a woman's role and **women's careers**
a man's shirt and **men's suits**

The same applies to nouns that don't change at all between singular and plural.
The apostrophe is always placed before the s̲, irrespective of the number of
things involved. Here there is no way of telling whether singular or plural is
intended either from hearing the words or seeing them written. **The deer's
antlers** could refer to one animal or a whole herd, while **a wolf in sheep's
clothing** might be wearing the fleece of one animal or, more likely, that of
several. (It would always be incorrect to write deers' or sheeps'.) This is a
small but genuine ambiguity in English usage; not one to lose sleep over,
though.

APOSTROPHES IN PROPER NOUNS
Names (proper nouns) which already end in s̲ generally add an apostrophe and
an additional s̲ in the possessive, particularly where the words are of only one
syllable:

Some of Charles's possessions are stolen in a break-in at St James's Palace

(Sun prediction for the next year)

Comparing his hairstyle with John Mills's in Ryan's Daughter was fairly typical.

(The Times)

With names of two or more syllables, practice varies.

Dickens's characters... are pure gold.

(Guardian)

Jesus's pallor makes his face shine.

(The Times)

(but you will also find **Dickens'** and **Jesus'** without the additional s)

The house style of most publishers (i.e. the system of punctuation, etc. adopted by a publishing house to ensure uniformity in its output) tends to be 's for modern names (Charles's; James's, etc.) but not for classical or Biblical ones where the apostrophe stands by itself (Moses'; Euripides'; Jesus').

Some well-known companies tend to exclude the apostrophe: e.g. Dixons, Barclays Bank, Lloyds Bank (but the City of London insurance company is Lloyd's).

AVOIDING THE APOSTROPHE

There is a convention that it is better to avoid using the apostrophe when referring to objects, i.e. when mentioning one thing that 'belongs' to another inanimate thing. Rephrasing with *of* is preferable, not because it is wrong to use the apostrophe but because the longer phrase is usually more euphonious – it sounds better!

the roof of the car instead of **the car's roof**

the cover of the book instead of **the book's cover**

the front of the building instead of **the building's front**

INCORRECT APOSTROPHES

Mistaken uses of the apostrophe include:

1) Inserting the apostrophe in a plural noun which is not in the possessive form:

✗✗ FULL-TIME BARTENDER'S REQUIRED

(pub notice in Reading)

(should be **BARTENDERS**. This would only be right if the notice read something like... **BARTENDER'S HELP REQUIRED...** if one individual was wanted;... **BARTENDERS' HELP...** if it was more than one).

✗✗ **DISABLED DRIVER'S ONLY**
>   *(road sign in the city of Bath)*

(should be **DRIVERS**)

✗✗ **... after 20 years' at the heart of the Conservative Party ...**
>   *(Observer)*

(should be **20 years**)

✗✗ **We can save Ian Sproat the trouble (and the taxpayers' their cash).**
>   *(Sun)*

(if **their** was left out the phrase would read correctly **the taxpayers' cash** but, as it stands, the apostrophe is wrongly included).

The exception to this rule (that an apostrophe should not be used with a straightforward plural which is not a possessive) comes with abbreviated words and numbers.

The presence of the apostrophe in shortened plurals like MP's, CD's, GCSE's is an arguable extra. The tendency is to omit the apostrophe (MPs, CDs, GCSEs), particularly in print.

The apostrophe is more likely to be preserved, however, when it comes to single numbers or single letters:

The way he writes his capital I's makes them look like 7's.

2) Another common mistake is putting the apostrophe after the s̲ in an irregular plural form. The apostrophe should always go <u>before</u> the s̲ in these cases:

✗✗ **Mens' cosmetics are an expanding part of the business.**

3) It is always wrong to include the apostrophe at the end of a possessive pronoun such as 'yours' or 'his', or in the third person singular present tense of a verb:

✗✗ **"...a modern state such as our's..."**
>   *(quoted, The Times)*

✗✗ **BAR-B-QUE PACK FEED'S 5**
>   *(shop sign)*

4) Sometimes the apostrophe is left out altogether, and it's not immediately clear whether the noun is in the singular or the plural:

✗ **It's the cats whiskers.**
>   *(mobile phone advertisement)*

(how many cats does it take to provide the whiskers?)

✗ After the surfers death, hundreds of people came to see the breakers.
   (The Times)

(singular **death** suggests that report is talking about one surfer and the rest of the item confirms that, but correct placing of the apostrophe, **surfer's,** would have avoided the ambiguity).

Even where there is no doubt about the meaning it is still incorrect to leave out the apostrophe in phrases such as **three years' time** or **one hour's work**:

✗ We are giving away one months supply of RESTORE hair growth formula...
   (Advertisement)

[should be **one month's**]

✗ £170 for five hours emergency labour on your car in France.
   (AA advertisement)

[should be **five hours'**]
   ⇨ (See also ITS / IT'S; WHO'S / WHOSE)

MISSING LETTERS

The apostrophe also marks where letters have disappeared, in the shortened phrases we use constantly:

   He (wi)ll / He'll; I (ha)ve / I've; Who (i)s there? / Who's there?;

   It (i)s me / It's me, etc

The apostrophe is placed where the missing letter would go rather than in the space between two words, so the following should read DIDN'T:

✗✗I DID'NT GET WHERE I AM TODAY BY HAVING THE VISION THING
   (cartoon caption, Independent on Sunday)

These shortened phrases, termed contractions or elisions, are almost universally used in spoken English, except where the speaker is being formal or emphatic (as, for example, in Winston Churchill's war-time speech: 'we shall fight them in the fields and in the streets, we shall fight in the hills...').

   Apostrophes should also be used to show where letters have been dropped at the beginning, middle or end of a word:

   huntin', shootin' and fishin'
   It's only rock 'n' roll
   reg'd; bos'n; 12 o'clock
   KNOCK 'EM BACK   *(Daily Star headline)*

In writing, letters are omitted either for convenience and brevity (as **reg'd**) or in a sometimes hip, informal approximation to the way people speak (**rock 'n' roll**). The acceptability of this varies widely. Of the examples given above only **bos'n** and **12 o'clock** would be found in formal writing. The others would be found in colloquial journalism, advertisements and other kinds of 'off duty' prose, such as reported speech in fiction:

> **"Drivin' down there as soon's I get up inna mornin', and then drivin' back up again, afternoons, and I'm drivin' the cab all night too. I admit I was gettin' pretty-near beat. It was really knockin' me out."**
>
> *(George V. Higgins, Bomber's Law)*

Some shortened word forms are so familiar in their abbreviated form that the apostrophe is no longer required: fridge; flu; phone; plane. It would look pedantic to put 'plane (if the context is formal, use aeroplane). It would look fossilised to write 'bus. With shortened numbers the tendency is to omit the apostrophe at the beginning, but both forms are perfectly acceptable in any type of writing except the most formal:

> **I grew up in the 60s**
>
> *(or '60s – but 1960s in formal use).*

⇨ (See also ELISIONS)

APPRAISE / APPRISE

The verb *appraise* is to <u>sum up</u>, to <u>estimate the value or quality of</u> something (not usually in a monetary context):

> **A few seconds in the room were sufficient for him to appraise the situation.**

(The noun is *appraisal* – a bit of a buzzword in the workplace where it is used to describe the process by which the strengths and weaknesses of employees are assessed by more or less sympathetic superiors.)

To *apprise* (formal rather than in everyday use) is to <u>give notice to</u>, <u>tell</u>:

> **He apprised me of what had happened in my absence.**

AROUSE / ROUSE

The verbs are almost interchangeable. To *arouse* is to <u>excite</u>, to <u>provoke</u>:

> **The proposal to build a by-pass aroused controversy.**

(The associated noun, *arousal*, frequently has a sexual application.)

To *rouse* is to <u>awaken</u>, to <u>stir up</u>:

> **The church bells roused him from his sleep.**

(A speech, song, etc. is to be described as *rousing*, not *arousing*.)

AS IF / LIKE

The use of *like* for *as if* or *as though* is very frequent:

She looked like she had some good news to tell.

(rather than... **as if she had...**).

The habit has spread from spoken (American) English to written English:

... we have stockpiled Kellogg's Corn Flakes like nuclear war was imminent ...

(Independent)

I felt like I was in a submarine.

(Michael Crichton, Rising Sun)

Using *like* in this way can cause ambiguity if the word is at first understood in one of its other senses of <u>similar to</u>:

It's not like the heritage of performers who direct is a wretched one ...

(Guardian)

Like in this sense of *as if* is still an informal usage, and its American flavour can suggest a strenuous desire on the part of the user to be seen as modish, laid-back prose-wise.

⇨ (See also LIKE)

ASSUME / PRESUME

There is no real difference between these verbs in the sense of to <u>take for granted</u>:

You speak the language so I assume / presume you'll be able to find your way around all right.

As nouns, the words diverge slightly. An *assumption* can be a <u>supposition which isn't supported by evidence</u>; 'false' is the adjective often partnered with it. A *presumption* has more the sense of a <u>probability</u>. Under English law, courts work on the *presumption* of innocence.

Another sense attached to *presumption* is <u>arrogance, insolence</u>:

... to write a biography is to make another's life your property – a colossal piece of presumption.

(The Times)

ASSURE / ENSURE / INSURE

The three verbs are related but have different applications. To *assure* is to <u>guarantee</u>, to <u>give certainty</u>:

They did their best to assure him that he was welcome.

To *ensure* is to <u>make safe or certain</u>:

Overwhelming numbers and superior firepower ensured victory.

To *insure* is to <u>protect oneself (financially) against loss or damage</u>:

We've insured the baggage after last year's disaster.

(The noun *assurance*, when used in the context of the insurance market, relates to those policies which cover an individual's life and pay the beneficiaries on his or her death. *Insurance* can also be used to describe [life] *assurance* policies, and is applied to everything else against which one can insure: accident, fire, theft, etc.)

ASTERISK

The asterisk (*) signals a foot-note to a page or a reference to information at the end of the chapter or the whole book. The second footnote on a single page may be indicated by a double asterisk (**). A third point can be indicated by the dagger device called the obelus (†).

After that, except in the most scholarly contexts, the text is in danger of being crowded out by the footnotes.

Like the dash and elliptical dots, the asterisk is also commonly used to indicate where letters have been omitted from obscenities that could offend the reader:

He responded with a fax saying, "** off, you crazy old dyke."**
(The Times)

(The star-burst effect of the asterisks may, paradoxically, draw the reader's attention to what has been left out rather than tactfully sliding over it.)
⇨ (See also DASH; ELLIPTICAL DOTS)

AURAL / ORAL

Both words are adjectives with a near-identical pronounciation (the first syllable rhyming with 'more').

Aural means of the ear. *Oral* means relating to the mouth, and, as a noun, describes an examination where the candidate makes spoken answers. Confusion sometimes arises when the words are used in the context of tests. An *aural* examination in French would be a test of a candidate's ability to hear and understand that language when spoken.

But a French *oral* tests the candidate's capacity to speak the language.

(Some speakers distinguish between the two words by pronouncing the first syllable of *aural* to rhyme with 'how'.)

AUTHORISED / AUTHORITARIAN / AUTHORITATIVE

All three of these adjectives are connected to the noun *authority*. *Authorised* means proper, permitted by recognised authority:

The inspectors made an authorised visit to the nuclear plant.

The word is often tagged to biographical revelations, where it suggests that the author has been given access to the subject's life, secrets and all.
(Paradoxically, the opposite term *unauthorised* is often used as a selling point since the word hints that you will discover things the subject would have preferred to keep hidden. In this sense *unauthorised* is a euphemism for

scandalous, dirt-searching.)

Authoritarian defines an attitude or style of rule <u>in which obedience to authority is rated more highly than individual freedom</u>. Noun or adjective, it can be applied to an individual or to an entire culture:

> **Communism threw up two of the 20th century's most authoritarian rulers: Stalin and Mao Tse-Tung.**

Authoritative means <u>possessing authority</u>, and is applied to individuals and sources which can be relied on to produce the right answer:

> **You can almost believe a timetable when it is printed in authoritative type.**
>
> *(Independent)*

AVERSE

⇨ See ADVERSE

BAIL / BALE

Bail is a noun and verb with several meanings. An accused person will obtain *bail*, or be *bailed*, in court, i.e. <u>gain release from custody before trial by providing some security</u> (usually financial) which will be forfeit if the defendant disappears.

Cricket stumps are topped by *bails*.

To *bail* also means to <u>clear water out</u> of something, and <u>to parachute out of an aircraft</u>.

Bale can also be used as a verb in these last two senses (*baling* water; *baling* out of a crashing aircraft). As a noun *bale* means a <u>bundle</u> (a *bale* of cotton); as a verb, <u>to do up in bundles</u> (*baling* hay).

BASICALLY

Basically, meaning <u>at bottom</u>, <u>fundamentally</u>, is acceptable in a sentence where it actually has a job to do:

> **For all the public posturing there were, basically, few differences between the two sides.**

But *basically* often adds nothing to a statement, and particularly when it is placed at the start of a sentence it may be no more than the verbal equivalent of a hand banged on the table: listen to me! Leave *basically* out wherever it is not absolutely required:

> ✘ **Basically, you can count the number of worthwhile westerns made between 1965 and 1975 on the fingers of one hand...**
>
> *(Independent)*

BETWEEN YOU AND I

⇨ See PRONOUNS

BILLION

There used to be a distinction between a billion in British English, where it means a million million (1,000,000,000,000), and a billion in American English, where it means a thousand million (1,000,000,000). The distinction remains, but in everyday use British English has adopted the American definition. When, say, trade deficits or the population of the world are given in billions, it is thousands of millions that are meant – luckily for trade, luckily for the world.

BORN / BORNE

Borne is the past participle form of the verb *to bear*. It is applied to the carrier or the thing or person carried:

Used to guns, he had borne arms almost from the time he learned to walk.

So we beat on, boats against the current, borne back ceaselessly into the past.

(Scott Fitzgerald, The Great Gatsby)

When *bear* is used in the sense of to give birth the form *borne* is used if the mother is the subject of the sentence:

She has borne four children.

Otherwise the correct form is *born*:

Four children were born to her.

Born in Rochester...

BOUGHT / BROUGHT

It's surprisingly easy to confuse the two words. *Bought* is the past participle form of *buy*; *brought* is the past participle of *bring*. If in doubt, check back to the root form of each verb.

BRACKETS

Curved brackets, also called parentheses, enclose information which is a kind of supplement to the rest of a sentence. A bracket never appears alone: once opened, a comment in parenthesis must be closed. At their simplest, brackets wrap up a fact, a date, a name:

...Ben Jonson's The Devil Is An Ass (1616) is a masterpiece...

... a loving if erratically functioning marriage between an army boffin

(played by Tommy Lee Jones) and his free-spirited wife (Lange) ...

(all quotations from <u>Guardian</u>)

Sometimes brackets contain an aside in which the writer wants to give an opinion without interrupting the overall flow of the sentence:

... and persuading the children (also well played) that mum may be mad...

... turns the present into a Donald Trump nightmare in Back To The Future II (is this worse than the real 1985?)...

Brackets can be used creatively, so that the information or opinion inside them somehow plays with what lies outside:

"It's a self-appreciation society for pompous windbags, people of a certain ilk who are into onanism, I should think." (Translation: wankers)

The bikers of *Mad Max* become thugs on jet-skis, who sometimes lie in ambush underwater (don't try this at home)..

Too frequent use of brackets makes for a clogged sentence, particularly if they're packed full of comment:

✘ **Some – notably James Toback (who included several films not unconnected to himself – 'Immodesty! Arrogance! Megalomania!'), Whit Stillman (who understandably felt duty-bound to nominate three great writers: Zavattini, Sturges and Wilder), and Donald Cammell ('Sorry I broke the rules – my usual problem!') – went way over the top numerically.**

(from a <u>Time Out</u> survey of '100 Best Films')

Everything is immaculately in place in this sentence, every dash, comma, quotation mark and so on, but there's too much information. The principal part of the sentence, **Some... went way over the top numerically,** is like a clothes line that's far too thin to support all the washing that's been hung from it.

The sentence that follows, though lengthy, works better because the material inside the brackets is simply illustrative rather than being a mixture of quotation, fact and comment:

Therefore, most time travel movies get side-tracked into comedy (how many times in the eighties did you hear the gag about the people from the past who didn't believe Ronald Reagan was president?) or action (Jean-Claude Van Damme scars baddie Ron Silver by wounding his younger doppelganger), suggesting Hollywood views past and future as playgrounds for movie stars and familiar genre formulae.

(Kim Newman, <u>Guardian</u>)

Punctuation which is applicable to the material inside the brackets – as the question mark in **(... who didn't believe Ronald Reagan was President?)** – should be included <u>within</u> those brackets. Punctuation marks which relate to the sentence as a whole go outside the <u>second</u> bracket, never the first. The

comma that occurs in **his younger doppelganger), suggesting...** separates the
word 'action' before the bracket from the clause beyond the bracket.

Brackets which contain a complete sentence stand independently of the
passage in which they occur, and all punctuation is placed inside the brackets:

> **... the £25 catalogue is so vast as to be... near unusable at the**
> **exhibition. (Another case for the Society for the Suppression of**
> **Self-indulgent Catalogues.)**
>
> *(Simon Jenkins, The Times)*

SQUARE BRACKETS

Square brackets are used by writers and editors when they are quoting
someone else's words and are adding their own aside or information:

> **"There is also the question of how many of our 800 [of which a quarter**
> **are first class] seats we could fill at that time."**

(comment about Eurostar train, quoted in the *Independent.* The words used by
the interviewee lie outside the square brackets; the reporter's comment comes
inside.)

> **'These are advantages which would turn to vast account, when we**
> **actually commenced a school [she wrote to Miss Branwell on 29**
> **September, 1841], and, if Emily could share them with me...'**

(letter from Charlotte Bronte, quoted by biographer Winifred Gerin)

Square brackets should also be used to contain information in a sentence or
portion of a sentence which is itself already in curved brackets. That sentence
might have been written as follows to illustrate the point: (Square brackets
should also be used when one pair of brackets is placed within another pair of
[curved] brackets.)

DIFFERENCE BETWEEN BRACKETS AND DASHES

Brackets and dashes are used fairly interchangeably, although brackets have
the edge in formality. If one can make any distinction, it is that brackets are
employed more for the conveying of information, while the material contained
between a pair of dashes often has the quality of a thrown-off aside:

> **Because they never do anything apart from write, authors are a**
> **sensitive lot – foresters are much nicer – and so grudges go deep.**
>
> *(Independent on Sunday)*

Brackets and dashes can be used together, as here:

> **My bright young work-shadow – fan of the Blur (and, as it happens,**
> **Michael Tippett) – passed when asked whether she had heard of**
> **Adullamites.**
>
> *(Philip Howard, The Times)*

(you feel that what's inside the brackets is to be taken a little more seriously
than the bit about Blur)

BROACH / BROOCH

Broach, a verb, generally occurs in two contexts: to *broach* a topic (i.e. to introduce it into conversation); and to *broach* a bottle (i.e. open it).

Brooch, a noun, is an ornamental clasp.

(Both words are pronounced in the same way, to rhyme with 'coach'.)

BUZZWORDS

Buzzwords are terms that catch the imagination of a substantial group of speakers / writers and become part of the general currency of the language. Buzzwords are an off-shoot of jargon (the key distinction is that they are more fashionable) and generally have their origin in a specialised area of activity. Business is a good source; among such terms are 'empowering', 'proactive', 're-engineering' 'delayering', 'downsizing', 'burnout'. Some of the words may have a metaphorical force ('burnout', for example, to signify exhaustion through intensive work), but others may be slightly obscure or euphemistic ('delayering' and 'downsizing' indicate getting rid of people at work).

⇨ (See also JARGON)

CAN or MAY?

Memories of being talked down to by adults may hang around this old distinction. When children once asked 'Can I leave the table?' they might be told that they could leave it, of course, but what they really meant was 'May I leave the table?' Although there is something pedantic about this correction, there are differences between the two verbs.

Can denotes ability: **She can speak five languages.** (but is often used informally in the sense of 'has permission': **She's just been told she can come on the trip.)**

May indicates possibility: **It may rain tomorrow** and permission: **You may leave when the job's finished.**

There is a small potential ambiguity in a sentence such as the one above (which could mean 'You might take it into your head to leave...'). There is a stronger ambiguity in a sentence like 'He may drive across.'

Context and delivery will tell the listener whether it's a matter of permission or of possibility.

⇨ (See also MAY / MIGHT)

CANNON / CANON

A *cannon* is a large gun or a type of shot in billiards.

Canon has a variety of applications:

> **a priest attached to a cathedral**
>
> **a principle or rule** *(as in 'accepted canons of decency')*

the body of work attributed to a particular author *(the Shakesperian canon, for example, covers all those works [plays and poems] generally considered to have been written by him and not attributable to another author).*

CANVAS / CANVASS

Canvas is <u>material used for painting on,</u> <u>for making ship's sails,</u> etc.

To *canvass* (verb) is to <u>establish other people's views</u> or to <u>gather support in a political setting</u>:

> **A week before Election Day, I went canvassing with my friend and neighbour Lisanne ...**
>
> *(Julian Barnes, Letters from London)*

Canvass also operates as a noun with the same sense of <u>estimating numbers, gathering support</u>. It should not be confused with the other word and spelling, as it is here:

> **✗✗...the first full canvas of Tory MPs suggested that Mr Major would win by a comfortable margin.**
>
> *(The Times)*

CAPITAL LETTERS AT THE BEGINNING OF A SENTENCE

A capital letter marks the start of a sentence, and must be used following a full stop – even if what comes next is technically not a sentence:

> **They'd better believe it. Because he means it.**
>
> *(Daily Star)*

DIRECT SPEECH

Capitals must be used at the start of direct speech, even when the words spoken do not begin the sentence as a whole:

> **...I found to my amazement that people kept hitting me on the shoulder and saying, "Who loves ya, baby?"**
>
> *(Miles Kington)*

The exception is when the identity of the speaker and the 'speech word' (such as 'shouted', 'whispered') breaks into what would otherwise be a single sentence when spoken. Then the next portion of the sentence starts with a lower case letter, not a capital:

> **"I know," he said, "but a split second before I was due to speak, I realised I had lost my card, so I had to improvise like Mad..."**
>
> *(Miles Kington)*

⇨ (see also PUNCTUATION IN DIRECT SPEECH)

PROPER NOUNS

Capitals are used for proper nouns – the names of individuals, countries, rivers, festivals like Christmas, large-scale sporting occasions, brand names, companies, etc:

...stand-in skipper Rob Andrew, the lone hero of England's shambling World Cup victory against Argentina...

(Daily Star)

Coca-Cola; Hoover; New Year; Thames

TITLES

principal words in the titles of books, plays, films, etc. are capitalised, a means of highlighting the items that are important because they carry the meaning. In practice this tends to apply to everything apart from some prepositions or conjunctions and the definite or indefinite article if it occurrs in the middle of the title:

Look Back in Anger

A Tale of Two Cities

Far From the Madding Crowd

From Russia, with Love

and there is a tendency with song and album titles to capitalise the whole thing:

... their landmark album, Dark Side Of The Moon...

... songs such as Let It Rain, Set Me Free and Hold My Body Tight...

(The Times)

FIRST PERSON SINGULAR

The first person singular (I) is always a capital (but not when in the object or possessive form – me, my / mine):

But I don't know who said it to me!

GOD

At one time not capitalising the deity of the Christian religion might have been thought a little daring, as well as ungrammatical. He should still be capitalised, unless you want to make a specific point by not doing so. It is still the practice to capitalise God when He occurs in pronoun form.

ABBREVIATIONS

Capitals are used for the abbreviated forms of organisations, countries, pressure groups and the like, when only the first letters of each word are used:

USA; AA; LA; BBC; BA; CNN; TUC; MP...

An abbreviation written out in full retains capitals for each word (except small connecting words that do not appear in the shortened form):

United States of America; Member of Parliament.

When the abbreviated words form a 'word' in their own right – and this only happens if the abbreviation can easily be pronounced as a single entity (none of the examples above falls into this category) – then a capital may be used for the initial letter only:

...the reinforcing troops would be wearing Unprofor [United Nations Protection Force] **blue berets...**

...after a Nato [North Atlantic Treaty Organisation] **foreign ministers' meeting yesterday...**

(Independent)

⇨ (see also ABBREVIATIONS; ACRONYMS; FULL STOPS)

NOTICES

If capitals are used in notices they should be used throughout, for every word: **KEEP OFF THE GRASS**. Alternatively a notice can be treated as a ordinary sentence and only the first word capitalised: **Thank you for not smoking**.

It is a mistake to capitalise the first letters of every word:

✖ **These Toilets Are Serviced And Inspected Regularly**

(motorway service station notice)

PLACES

Confusion sometimes arises over when to use capitals in titles, place names and geographical areas. When an ordinary noun becomes part of a title it should be capitalised:

He walked down the street *but* **He walked down Oxford Street**;

the kings of England *but* **King Richard II of England**.

Giving capitals to an important post or title usually indicates that the writer has a specific holder of that post in mind even if he or she is not named:

Now, can we hope that the Home Secretary will listen to his own research department...?

(Polly Toynbee, Independent)

Using lower case letters generally suggests that the writer has no particular individual in mind:

Any prime minister will have ups and downs in the polls.

COMPASS POINTS

Compass points should take capitals if their use in a place name or area forms a recognised entity:

The West; South America; East Indies; North Pole

but where they are used purely in an adjectival sense then capitals are unnecessary:

Power lines were brought down in southwest England and the South East suffered driving rain...

(The Times)

(the report could have read **in the South West**, omitting **England**, and paralleling the noun use of **South East**)

✗ **...they've launched the Institute of Higher Sexology from their council maisonette in Plumstead, South East London.**

(Daily Star)

(the name of the sex institute and the suburb are correctly capitalised, but **South East London** isn't an entity like, say, the **East End**. Should read **south-east / southeast London**.)

CHANGE OF MEANING

Putting a capital on some words changes their meanings. An individual may have conservative ideas without membership of the Conservative Party, be liberal in attitude without belonging to a political grouping such as the Liberal Democrats or possess catholic (i.e. wide-ranging) tastes without being part of the Catholic Church:

'A Catholic taste in food, I'd say, but if you put a good Yorkshire roast in front of him, he won't turn it down.'

(as quoted in the Independent on Sunday)

(An odd comment anyway since if you had a catholic taste in food you'd presumably be more than happy with Yorkshire pudding.)

CENSOR / CENSURE

As a verb *censor* is to check material so as to assess its suitability for 'publication' (this covers letters, film, TV, etc.). Wartime provides a natural context:

All the officer patients in the ward were forced to censor letters written by all the enlisted-men patients...

(Joseph Heller, Catch-22)

The person who does this is the *censor*. The best-known system of censorship in the UK is run by the British Board of Film Censors (BBFC).

To *censure* is to judge unfavourably, to rebuke:

The MP was censured for accepting money to ask a question in the House.

CENSORED / CENSORIOUS

Both words derive from *censor*. *Censored* describes a book, play, film, etc. from which material has been cut on grounds of taste, potential offensiveness and so on. The word also applies to the excluded material:

Fifteen seconds were censored from the film when it was shown on TV.

Censorious is an adjective meaning <u>fault-finding</u>, and carries with it an overtone of pettiness:

He enjoyed finding ways around the restrictions placed on smokers by an increasingly censorious society.

(The Times)

CENTENARY / CENTENNIAL

Centenary (noun and adjective) is a British English usage meaning a <u>hundred year anniversary</u>. *Centennial* is a rare adjective meaning <u>happening once in a hundred years</u>. However, the US noun usage of the term to mean a hundred-year anniversary, like *centenary*, (as in '1965 was the centennial of Abraham Lincoln's assassination.') is increasingly found in Britain.

CEREMONIAL / CEREMONIOUS

Both adjectives derive from *ceremony*.

Ceremonial means <u>with proper ceremony or ritual</u>:

After the treaty was signed, there was a ceremonial exchange of pens.

Ceremonious conveys a note of criticism and means <u>over-concerned with ceremony</u>:

His ceremonious manner made it clear that we were privileged to meet him.

CHILDISH / CHILDLIKE

There is a clear division between these two words – which, incidentally, aren't usually applied to children themselves. *Childish* is used about adults in a critical sense, and describes behaviour which is <u>non-adult</u>, <u>petulant</u>, <u>spoilt</u> – all the things which adults are supposed to have grown out of. *Childish* is the antithesis of 'grown-up'.

Even in his 30s he had childish tastes in food, preferring dishes that were bland or sweet.

Childlike is also applied to adults but this time with approval, as it characterises not so much behaviour, as responses such as surprise and delight;

or qualities like simplicity and trust – things that allegedly come more easily to children. *Childlike* is the opposite of 'worldly', 'cynical'.

> **Films by Steven Spielberg, such as ET, show a childlike wonder at what the universe may have in store for us.**

⇨ (see also MACHO / MANLY / MANNISH; WOMANISH / WOMANLY)

CHORD / CORD

A *chord* is a string of a musical instrument, and the spelling to use in sentences such as:

> **The opening chords of the symphony rang through the hall.**

Cord, in the sense of thick string, is the spelling that is usually applied in *spinal cord* (sometimes *spinal chord*) and always in *vocal cords*.

CLASSIC / CLASSICAL

The two words have a variety of applications. *Classic* indicates that whatever is being described is an outstanding example of its type or, at least, a highly representative one: a book, film, song, dress, car – even a remark or a mistake may be classic.

Classic is adjective or noun:

> **The miniskirt was a classic example of 1960s clothes design.**

> **The Russian novel Dr Zhivago is a 20th century classic.**

Use of the word tends to suggest not only that the object in question is good, the product of great skill, loving attention, etc. but also that a certain amount of time has gone by since its creation – for *classic* status is usually achieved over a period rather than being arrived at in a day. However, reference to an 'instant classic' is quite common, and the term may describe something that earns laughter rather than admiration. A newspaper offered prizes in a Seventies' Style Classics competition which included a 'gold double Jacuzzi and British Racing green toilet with gold glitter seat' (one-time property of Elton John). Tongue-in-cheek *classic*.

As a plural noun, the term *the classics* generally carries a dignified weight; it is applied to works of art (most frequently literature and music created before 1900) which have lasted and achieved the kind of status that makes references to them the intellectual equivalent of touching wood.

The Classics, usually capitalised, refer to the literature and culture of ancient Greece and Rome, and more particularly to their study in school or university.

Classical is an adjective describing anything relating to the Roman and ancient Greek period – history, literature, studies. But it is also used about more recent cultural products, particularly in music and architecture, until the early 19th century. In this sense it points towards a certain formality and order (this is the link with the Roman / Greek application) and is usually contrasted with the more exuberant term romantic. In this piece of cultural pigeon-holing,

Johann Sebastian Bach (1685-1750) is a *classical* composer, and Johannes Brahms (1833-97) a *romantic* one.

In music history there is a more restricted and specialist application of *classical* to describe music composed between c.1750 and 1800 by the likes of Haydn, Mozart, and Beethoven.

The word, particularly in a musical context, is very elastic. So any music which is not pop (in its widest sense) is often described as *classical*. And the following may give an idea of the extensive application of *classical* and how it can be distinguished from *classic*.

Benjamin Britten (1913-76) wrote 20th century *classical* music (and *classics*); John Lennon and Paul McCartney wrote 20th century *classics* (but not *classical* music).

CLICHÉ

A cliché is an expression which has turned stale through overuse:

fish out of water

break new ground

take on board

back with a vengeance

from day one

a whole new ball game

a level playing-field

men of violence

state of the art

There are other phrases, which one might term 'marginal clichés', where the same noun and adjective are frequently coupled:

nagging doubt

categoric denial

emotional appeal

shrewd suspicion

lethal cocktail

mass exodus

hopeless case

Sebastian Faulks, writing in the <u>*Guardian*</u>, provided a witty commentary on the attraction some words hold for each other:

' **"Unfailing" is an adjective that took secret marital vows to the noun "courtesy" in the register office of popular English usage. Their brief ceremony followed that of "staunch" to "Conservative" and "dire" to "straits". The couple are now seldom seen without each other in public.'**

These expressions, often metaphorical, have lost most of the colour and energy they once possessed. We're so used to cliché that we remain unaware (or in clichéd terms 'blissfully ignorant') of the striking, sometimes bizarre undertones of phrases like 'happy hunting-ground' or 'on cloud nine' or 'ride roughshod over'. A cliché can be revived by being given a humorous, or ironic, aptness:

He would not have been appointed by Mrs Thatcher if Whitehall had feared his track record might have encouraged him to run off the rails.

(Guardian obituary of former British Rail chief, so 'track record' and 'run off the rails')

Much prose comes pre-packaged, like a kitchen cabinet. The writer has reached for the nearest hand-me-down phrases. Inevitably, journalism, with its tight deadlines and awareness that today's words are unlikely to be studied in much detail tomorrow, inclines towards the cliché:

Still, that is now water under the bridge; division of the spoils is now the order of the day.

(Independent)

That begged one question – and not solely how much damage the free-flowing Samoans can cause. More importantly, what will happen to England's suddenly struggling defence when the big guns of Australia and New Zealand get their hands on them?

(Sun)

Equally, newspapers provide some mildly witty variations on cliché, particularly in headlines and sub-headings:

The drivers with a bee under their bonnet

Dressed to skill

Two's company, but three's a photo call.

It is almost impossible to prevent clichés surfacing in what we say and write. The joke advice to 'Avoid clichés like the plague' neatly illustrates the problem. While one couldn't (and shouldn't) search for a fresh and original way of saying everything – conversation would be impossible if one did, and writing would be painful for writer and reader both – a paragraph or a speech which is constructed entirely out of the building blocks of cliché suggests a certain insensitivity to language.

⇨ (See also IDIOM in *Glossary*)

CLIMATIC / CLIMACTIC

Two adjectives with completely different meanings. *Climatic* is the adjective from climate:

Climatic change may be an early sign of global warming.

Climactic is the adjective from climax:

At the climactic moment of Tchaikovsky's 1812 Overture the audience hears the sound of imitation cannon fire.

COHERENT / COHESIVE

Both adjectives derive from *cohere*, to stick together. *Coherent* means connected, making sense and is a term of mild approval for the logic of a speech, argument, etc. It often occurs in a negative context:

The lecturer lost his notes and his demonstration was hardly coherent.

Cohesive means having the power to unite, sticking together:

The new captain moulded the side into a cohesive team.

COLON

A colon (:) separates a sentence into different but related sections:

The OJ trial is over: has justice been done and been seen to be Done?
(The Times)

A colon has the effect of pulling the reader up more sharply than a comma would do:

Here is the news: BBC will open its doors to tourists
(The Times headline)

and can give the 'explanation' that follows it something of the quality of a punchline:

But the family of at least one old man in the picture was none too pleased to see it being used again in a different context: not least because he died some years ago.
(Private Eye)

A colon can also be used when the halves of the sentence which it separates are balanced:

Her book is definitely this year's collector's item: rather in the way that Major Major by the Prime Minister's brother, Terry, was last year's.
(The Times)

(a comma could have been used here, but would not have given to the two parts of this sentence quite the same 'equally matched' feel).

A colon is frequently used to mark a quotation or a piece of speech (particularly in the absence of an introductory 'said', etc.):

... she shakes with laughter at the duchess's plight: "A horrible old lady locked up by another horrible old lady."

The colon may be used to introduce a list:

The following countries are the permanent members of the United

Nations Security Council: America, Britain, China, France, Russia.

(The use of the colon in such a context suggests that the list is comprehensive rather than selective.)

When what follows after the colon is a complete and distinct sentence, but not a piece of direct speech, a capital letter can be used to introduce that sentence:

That's the problem with today's leadership contest: No one knows who's going to vote for whom.

(Sun)

⇨ (See also SEMI-COLON and DIFFERENCES BETWEEN COLON & SEMI-COLON)

COMIC / COMICAL

The words are close but not identical in their applications. As an adjective *comic* suggests that what it describes is intended to amuse (*comic* song, *comic* double act). As a noun *comic* is synonymous with 'comedian'.

Comical, an adjective, means laughable – but not necessarily by intention:

His attempts to play the tragic hero were comical.

COMMA

Commas are the written equivalent of very short pauses in speech, and if they are inserted where one would stop, briefly, on reading something aloud, then their placing will be more or less accurate. Their use is not arbitrary. Commas clarify the meaning of the words they come between. Consider the difference which a comma makes in the following sentences:

i) Yesterday, he said he was the happiest man in the world.

(He made this statement yesterday; the implication is that he is still the happiest man in the world.)

ii) Yesterday, he said, he was the happiest man in the world.

(He made this statement today; the implication is that, while he was the happiest man in the world twenty-four hours ago, things are different today.)

Whether or not to put in a comma is sometimes optional, but there are still guidelines about their use. Some follow:

a) Commas are used to separate items in a list of nouns:

... with art paper tickling smooth to the touch and a smell of corresponding richness, with jokes, stories, photographs, quizzes, puzzles, and prizes for competitions which the Tulsi children were all going to enter but never would...

(V S Naipaul, A House for Mr Biswas)

The comma before the final 'and' in such a list [**puzzles, and prizes**] is optional, and is more often omitted, particularly where the list is relatively short:

They bought onions, peppers, aubergines, tomatoes and garlic.

However, for the sake of clarity a comma needs to be included if an item at or near the end of the list already contains an 'and':

Tomorrow's forecast promises mist, rain, thunder and lightning, and some sun at the end of the day.

Where an 'and' phrase forms a separate parenthetical-style comment in a list it should be enclosed in commas at beginning and end:

...one of the country's most successful, and best-loved, comedians.

(The Times)

✘ (This would be incorrect if the second comma were omitted ... **most successful, and best-loved comedians.**)

b) Commas also separate a series of verbs / actions:

He ran, walked, staggered, almost crawled, but he got to the finishing line.

c) As a very general rule it is optional to use commas when dealing with a list of adjectives coming before a noun:

a large, old, dilapidated house / a large old dilapidated house

When the adjectives follow a noun or pronoun they must be separated by commas:

The house was large, old, dilapidated.

⇨ (See also ADJECTIVES)

d) Commas mark off phrases and clauses:

And it was at this time, some six months later, that Moti came to the shop and rapped hard on the counter.

(V S Naipaul)

Note that the entire phrase **some six months later** is enclosed in commas, which here function like brackets or dashes. The phrase could be lifted out of the sentence without altering the sense of the principal thing that the writer is saying. It would be incorrect to place only one comma.

Failure to put commas in at the begining <u>and</u> end of a phrase leads to confusion, however mild:

✘ **Adjacent to the beach, this holiday park with the fabulous Embassy Club and all the fun of the fair, is perfect for holdays with the family.**

(caravan park advertisement)

(Either the second comma, after **fair**, should be omitted or an extra one put in after **holiday park**.)

e) A comma should mark the beginning or end of direct speech when used with a speech word like 'said', 'shouted', 'whispered':

One evening Seth said, 'That tin of Ovaltine could very well be your last, if you don't decide to do something.'

When the identity of the speaker comes afterwards, the comma goes <u>inside</u> the quotation mark:

'A man like Mungroo should be in jail,' Moti said.

(V S Naipaul)

⇨ (See also PUNCTUATION IN DIRECT SPEECH)

f) Commas must be used with some relative clauses:

The trees in the park, which wasn't much visited, looked beautiful.

but not all (see THAT / WHICH and WHICH / ,WHICH for discussion of difference between defining and descriptive clauses).

g) Care needs to be taken over the placing of the comma near the beginning of a sentence. There is a difference in meaning between:

Now there were some things he couldn't accept.

(where 'now' signifies 'at the present time') and

Now, there were some things he couldn't accept.

(where 'now' followed by the comma signifies that some new point is being taken up by the speaker or writer).

h) The comma isn't a universal item of punctuation, able to plug any pause in writing. Excessive reliance on commas can produce a slightly awkward or confusing tone:

The rich are different, a detail some of them ignore, avoiding the status symbols, such as private bank accounts, pukka brokers, and platinum cards, that mark out wealth to the rest of the world.

(The Times)

(Leaving out the comma after **brokers** would have made this read better. Better still would be some variation in punctuation that avoided a sequence of six commas: use of a colon or a dash, for example.)

Inserting commas can change or impair a writer's meaning:

✖ **There are some very unpleasant men, indeed, in** [the film] ***Casino.***

(The Times)

('indeed' is intended to reinforce 'very unpleasant'; instead, because it is insulated from the rest of the sentence by the pair of commas, it operates less as an adverb and more as an interjection expressing something like surprise: very unpleasant men – really?)

COMMON / MUTUAL

The difference between these two is nicely illustrated in:

The common ground Castleford, Wakefield and Featherstone Rovers, the third party, share is mutual loathing ...

(The Times)

Common means shared, held jointly, as in common knowledge. *Mutual* describes something which is reciprocated; in the example, a feeling of loathing which each of the three teams involved in the Rugby League gives out and receives back from the other two. But *mutual* is also used in the sense of held in common, as in the title of Dickens's *Our Mutual Friend*, and this is a usage which has long found general acceptability. In fact, had Dickens called the novel *Our Common Friend* the title would have been ambiguous.

COMPARE / CONTRAST

To *compare* is to put things side by side and look for similarities:

She compared their faces and could see many traces of the father in the son.

To *contrast* is to look for differences:

He contrasted the crude forgery with the genuine article.

Compare to and *compare with* have different applications. *Compare to* means to liken:

'Shall I compare thee to a summer's day?'

(first line of Shakespeare sonnet)

Compare with has more the sense of to look for what is similar and different:

We compared last year's brochure prices with this year's.

COMPELLING / COMPULSIVE / COMPULSORY

The adjectives *compelling* and *compulsive* are close in meaning when applied to experiences or processes: a *compelling* or *compulsive* book or TV programme is a highly readable or viewable one.

When applied to a person, *compulsive* is a pejorative term: a *compulsive* thief, a *compulsive* liar. This kind of *compulsion* comes from within the individual.

By contrast, *compulsory* (never used to describe an individual) describes something that one is made to do by regulation, a stronger force outside oneself:

Some employers are adopting compulsory drugs tests for their workforces.

COMPLEMENT / COMPLIMENT

The two words are both nouns and verbs. The one letter difference, and their identical pronunciation, might have been designed for confusion. As a noun the *complement* is the addition which will make for rightness or wholeness:

For the British, chips are the right complement to fried fish.

The verb *to complement* describes the process of adding something to make complete:

Almond's tight bouffant perfectly complemented the stripped-down primal throb of the duo's music ...

   (Guardian)

Compliment, noun or verb, is praise:

She complimented him on his skill in cooking.

The usual mistake is to use this word when the other (the 'e' one) is intended:

✗✗ **The first of two movies being shown to compliment the Wild West** [season] ...

   (Independent)

But in these examples the writers meant *compliment* and used the other one:

✗✗ **"She is not particularly good-looking," he says as straightforwardly as if he was complementing her.**

   (The Times)

✗✗ **...the ultimate Yorkshire complement: "This one's not bad."**

   (Independent)

COMPREHENSIBLE / COMPREHENSIVE

Comprehensible describes something that can be understood, and is usually applied to speech:

His words were so slurred that he was barely comprehensible.

Comprehensive means inclusive:

She gave a comprehensive account of all she'd done since we last saw her.

Both words are adjectives. (There is a noun use of *comprehensive* to define the type of school that is inclusive in its intake, i.e. does not discriminate between pupils on academic or other grounds.)

COMPRISE / CONSIST

These two verbs have more or less the same meaning, both being to do with the elements that make up a whole, but *consist* is always followed by 'of' or 'in':

His preparations for the one-man trip up the Amazon consist of packing his swimming trunks and writing his will.

but:

The New Testament comprises 27 books.

'Comprises of' is often found but still wrong:

✗ 'Over half of the building is actually comprised of thatched roof.'
   (Another Foot in the Past, BBC2)

CONCAVE / CONVEX

Something which is *concave* curves inward, while a *convex* object curves outward. ('*Concave* caves in' is a helpful way of remembering which is which.)

CONTEMPTIBLE / CONTEMPTUOUS

Both adjectives derive from *contempt* but have different applications. *Contemptible* means vile, worthy of contempt:

The efforts of the accused to shift the blame from himself to others were contemptible, said the judge.

Contemptuous decribes a person who shows contempt, is scornful:

She was openly mocking or contemptuous of anything she regarded as weakness.

⇨ (See also DERISIVE / DERISORY)

CONTINUOUS / CONTINUAL

Continuous means occurring without interruption:

We had continuous rain for 24 hours.

Continual also indicates something lasting over a period but with breaks or interruptions:

The council's budget is subject to continual cut-backs.

CORD

⇨ See CHORD

COULD OF

'Could of' as in:

✗✗ They could of taken the alternative road.

is always wrong, as are 'would of', 'might of' and 'should of'. The mistake is a written version of what we hear: 'They could've...'.

'Could've', 'would've' and 'should've' ought to be used only in informal writing.

(But the spellings '...could / would / should of...' might appear in dialogue in a story to indicate the way the words are actually pronounced. Such spellings can only be used, however, within the kind of diplomatic immunity provided by quotation marks.)

⇨ (See also DIALOGUE; ELISIONS)

COUNCIL / COUNSEL

A *council* is an official group of people; it is a noun only and is most often found in the context of local government:

> **It would be wrong to smear all Labour councils ...**
>
> *(Sun)*

Someone who serves on such a *council* is a *councillor*.

Counsel is both a noun and a verb and carries the sense of advice / se, often with a professional aspect:

> **A doctor for over 30 years, she could be relied on to give good counsel to newly qualified GPs.**
>
> **Their solicitor counselled them to let the matter drop.**

Such advice, particularly if it is of a therapeutic kind, is often referred to as *counselling*, and the person who gives it as a *counsellor*.

Counsel also has the more specialised meaning of courtroom lawyer:

> **Edward Carson, who had been counsel against Wilde in the libel case...**
>
> *(The Times)*

(The US variant of *counsel* in this sense [lawyer] is *counselor*.)

CREDIBLE / CREDITABLE / CREDULOUS

Credible means believable:

> **He had some extraordinary things to say but his quiet manner made them credible.**

The adjective is widely used now to suggest not so much that something exists (i.e., is not a fiction), but that it should be taken seriously:

> **The Bosnian government army has become a credible fighting force ...**
>
> *(Independent)*

(The associated noun is *credibility* with the sense of believabilty:

> **... the credibility for the policy of deterrence that thereafter kept the peace.**
>
> *(The Times)*

Creditable means worth praising, with the slight suggestion that

whatever is to be praised has been achieved in difficult circumstances:

> **Despite his ankle injury, the tennis player put up a very creditable performance.**

(The noun equivalent is *credit* with the sense of <u>honour</u>, <u>worth</u>, and frequently with a financial application, as in *credit* limit, etc.)

Credulous means <u>easily deceived</u>, <u>ready to accept whatever people say</u>:

Only a very credulous person would accept my proposal to sell him the Eiffel Tower.

(The associated noun, rarely used, is *credulousness*. <u>Credulity</u> has the same meaning and is more often found.)

CRITERION

Criterion, a noun meaning <u>a standard of judging</u>, is a singular word:

Academic excellence is the only criterion for entry.

The plural form is *criteria*:

Height and physical fitness are among the criteria for those wishing to join the police force.

It is incorrect to treat *criteria* as a singular noun:

✗✗ **The criteria for entry was never having been paid for a stand-up routine ...**

(The Times)

DASH

ONE DASH

A single dash acts like a colon or a comma, marking off a few words from the first part of the sentence:

Cedric's pay-off will be even more obscene than his salary – but worth every penny to Tricky Dicky.

(Private Eye)

Carefully used, and particularly when followed by one or two words only, the dash provides a little kick in the tail of a sentence:

BSkyB is aware that some of Capel's leading clients have decided not to invest in the shares – yet.

(The Times)

The historic landscapes of too much of west Suffolk are just that – relics.

(Independent on Sunday)

Neville has a problem as a writer – he cannot write.

(Guardian)

TWO DASHES

Two dashes used close together work like brackets and indicate this kind of parenthetical comment:

> **All of a sudden 'mooning' – the reprehensible practice of baring your bottom in public – has become an activity fraught with peril.**
>
> *(The Big Issue)*

It should be possible to remove whatever is inside the dashes and leave the rest of the sentence as a coherent whole. In other words, the information contained within the dashes may be amusing, interesting and so on – but it will not be vital for an understanding of what the writer means. In the following example the bits of the sentence on either side of the dashes don't easily match:

> ✘ **It is gratifying for any politician to press the button which brings applause – cheers, howls, tumultuous hand clapping, grown men in tears, delirium in the aisles – come splashing down the hall.**
>
> *(Guardian)*

The material that comes inside the dashes should not be so extensive that the reader gets lost and has to return to the start of the sentence to connect it to the end. In this example the words between the dashes create an interesting picture but they crowd out what should be the main part of the sentence (only six words):

> ✘ **Asbestos litigation lawyers – their pulses set racing by comments such as this from one former tenant: "If that had been a private landlord, I perhaps could have forgiven, but knowing that this was a council and knowing that we were vulnerable people, in the sense that we were homeless and we had a little child... allowing us to live with such danger is, to me, unforgivable..." – are standing by.**
>
> *(Independent)*

Wrongly placed dashes convey the wrong meaning:

> ✘✘ **The world's worst nuclear accident – until the Chernobyl disaster in 1986 – killed 33 men, scattering radioactivity over much of the Cumbrian countryside.**
>
> *(Independent)*

(This suggests that 33 men were killed in an earlier accident before Chernobyl. In fact, as a correction in the newspaper made clear a week later, it was Chernobyl that was responsible for the deaths. The dash should have come after **killed 33 men**, not before it, and the remainder of the sentence have been rewritten.)

Dashes which are placed close together but don't in fact mark a brackets-style comment can also be misleading because the writer is not enclosing information but merely breaking up a piece of prose:

> ✘ **...his definition of a statistician – someone who knows 99 ways of making love – but doesn't have a girlfriend.**
>
> *(The Times)*

(This would have been more accurate if a colon had followed 'statistician', making it clear that everything that came afterwards was a single statement).

MULTIPLE DASHES

Frequent use of the dash – not to enclose extra information but to interrupt prose writing – is generally inappropriate in formal English. There's a suspicion that it's a lazy writer's device. Sir Ernest Gowers in The Complete Plain Words, one of the old bibles of English usage, says: 'The dash is seductive; it tempts the writer to use it as a punctuation-maid-of-all-work that saves him the trouble of choosing the right stop.' However, the dash was once commonplace in diaries and letters, and can work very well in conveying urgency or a sketchy impression of a scene. Lord Byron (1788-1824), a prolific, hectic letter-writer, raised the dash to an art form:

> **Dearest Augusta – I returned home a few days ago from Rome – but wrote to you on the road – at Florence I believe – or Bologna – the last city you know – or do not know – is celebrated for the production of Popes – Cardinals – painters – & sausages –**
>
> *(Byron to his half-sister, 1817)*

DASHES FOR MISSING LETTERS

Dashes are also used to indicate missing letters, and can have a teasing quality. In the 19th century they would hint that the writer didn't want to reveal the exact location or date of his narrative (**the town of S –, the province of T –, in the year 18 –**).

Nowadays dashes are used by some newspapers to indicate obscenities which they are reluctant to print in full (asterisks are another substitute for the full-length word).

A dash can be suggestive. The reader supplies his or her own word in such cases. At least one novel ends with a dash. In 1768 Laurence Sterne concluded *A Sentimental Journey* like this:

> **So that when I stretched out my hand, I caught hold of the Fille de Chambre's -**

(The modern equivalent of this might be **the Fille de Chambre's ...** or, more likely, would tell us exactly what part of the Fille de Chambre had been caught hold of.)

DATES

The English convention in formal contexts (e.g. business letters) is to follow the day-month-year order, using numbers for the first and last part and spelling out the month in full: **8 July 1995.**

(This is now more usually found than **8th July 1995.**)

Numbers only can be used, particularly in less formal writing (e.g. memos):

8 / 7 / 95; but your correspondent should be working to the same order. American usage inverts the day and month: **7 / 8 / 95**.

An alternative, if unusual, way of numbering is to use a Roman numeral for the month: **8 – vii – 95**.

At least one organisation, the BBC, still uses Roman numerals on the copyright notice at the tail-end of the credit titles to give the year of production: MCMXCV. Cynics might wonder whether this is to hamper the viewer from realising exactly how long ago the programme was made. On the other hand, it might just be a classy way of signifying the date.

DECEITFUL / DECEPTIVE

The two adjectives, although related in meaning, are found in different contexts. *Deceitful* is used only about people or their behaviour and means intentionally misleading, false:

Using a forged ticket, he made a deceitful attempt to claim the prize.

Deceptive also means misleading, but not necessarily by intention:

The gloomy start was deceptive; the sun was out by mid-day.

DECIDED / DECISIVE

There is a considerable overlap between these two adjectives but also a difference of meaning in some contexts. Both carry the sense of firm: a *decided* rejection; a *decisive* individual.

Decided also means definite, unmistakable:

There was a decided edge to his voice when he talked about his schooldays.

Decisive also means having absolute influence (over the outcome):

Our captain's injuries gave the other side a decisive advantage.

(A *decided* advantage would be one that was clear-cut without being absolute.)

DEFINITE / DEFINITIVE

Definite means exact, not vague:

Have you got any definite plans for the summer?

Definitive means decisive, final:

Arguing over Scrabble, we looked to the dictionary for a definitive answer.

Definitive carries the additional sense of setting a standard:

Laurence Olivier's Richard III is regarded by many critics as the definitive interpretation.

DEFUSE / DIFFUSE

Defuse is found only as a verb and means, literally, <u>to take the fuse out</u> (of a bomb) or, figuratively, <u>to bring calm into a tense situation</u>:

That's to say, making his life more comfortable, but also defusing his violent tendencies.

(The Times)

Diffuse as a verb means <u>to scatter</u>, but it mainly occurs as an adjective in the sense of <u>spread over a wide area</u> or figuratively, as in the next example, with the sense of <u>imprecise</u>:

Diffuse plotting and too much blood mar the opening

(The Times)

The usual mistake is to put this second word where the first would be correct:

✗✗ Cade attempts to diffuse the situation in his usual diplomatic fashion...

(Telegraph)

✗✗ In a bid to diffuse the growing international row Tim Eggar... held a briefing for Dutch and German journalists Yesterday.

(The Times)

The two words are differently pronounced. *Defuse* takes a z-sound for the *s*, while *diffuse* has a sibilant-sounding *s* (-ss-).

DELUSION

⇨ See ALLUSION

DEPENDANT / DEPENDENT

Dependant is a noun only and describes <u>someone who depends on another for support</u> (usually financial):

She had four dependants, including her aged mother.

Dependent is an adjective meaning <u>contingent</u>, <u>relying on</u>:

The college place is dependent on his results.

(*Independent* has only one spelling whether it is used as a noun or a adjective: he stood as an *independent*; an *independent* analysis.)

DEPRECATE / DEPRECIATE

Deprecate is more forceful than the similar-looking verb *depreciate*, and means <u>to disapprove strongly of</u>, <u>to protest against</u>:

Total strangers saw fit to deprecate him, with the result that he was

stricken early with a guilty fear of people...

(Joseph Heller, Catch-22)

The adjective *self-deprecating* has the milder sense of <u>self-disparaging</u>, and suggests a modesty which is sometimes tactical:

The Oscar-winner gave a self-deprecating speech in which he credited everyone but himself with his award.

To *depreciate* is <u>to go down in value</u>, the opposite of 'appreciate'.

Most cars depreciate the moment they are driven out of the showroom.

It also carries the sense of <u>run down</u>, <u>disparage</u>:

No car salesman is likely to depreciate his own products.

DERISIVE / DERISORY

Although the two adjectives receive broadly the same definition in many dictionaries (<u>scoffing</u>), there is a difference in their usage.

Derisive means <u>showing humorous contempt for</u>:

There was a wall composed of transparent sacks full of fiery carrots. They looked at me like derisive faces ...

(Iris Murdoch, The Black Prince)

To describe something as *derisory* means that it is absurdly inadequate and can justifiably be treated with a dismissive laugh. The adjective almost invariably occurs in a financial context: to describe pay rises, football transfer offers, etc.:

Another factor was the derisory offer from Inter. They bid only £2 million.

(Daily Mirror)

⇨ (See also CONTEMPTUOUS / CONTEMPTIBLE)

DESERT / DESSERT

The *desert* is a dry sandy place (Sahara, Kalahari) while *deserts* (in the plural) are <u>what one deserves</u>. The term almost always has a negative ring. To get your *deserts*, almost inevitably *just deserts*, is to receive your <u>comeuppance</u>, the unpleasant consequences of your actions. *Dessert* is the last course in a meal. In the following clipping what the film apparently received from its audience was the pudding:

✗✗ At least Jim Jarmusch's existential western _Dead Man_ got its just desserts from the audience: glum faces and a sprinkling of shallow laughter.

(The Times)

DEVICE / DEVISE

Device is the noun spelling:

He was able to calculate the power of the device.

(The Times)

while *devise* is the verb:

They devised a simple plan.

⇨ (see also PRACTICE / PRACTISE, etc.)

DIALECT

Dialect is the form of language, spoken or (less often) written, which is used in a particular region of a country and whose use marks out the people from that region. Dialect shows itself in the way words are pronounced as well as in the choice of words themselves. Dialect is distinguished from standard English, and was traditionally regarded as a deviation from a norm, as less correct. Among linguists and writers on language there is now a healthy dialect defence group ready to spring to the protection of these forms of the language which are seen as having an energy and a validity that may sometimes be stronger than the middle-of-the-road formalities of standard English.

Almost all writing, from newspapers to advertisements, is presented in standard English. Standard English is the norm for speech in the media, and people's conservatism is shown by the fact that the strongly marked regional accent of a radio or television presenter, let alone the use of dialect, will be remarked on. Dialect is sometimes found in dialogue in fiction, and occasionally in direct quotation in newspaper articles and so on. Using dialect challenges readers – because they have to engage with a style of language which will be unfamiliar, unless they happen to share the author's background – but it also gives a particular authenticity to what's being said.

Strange thing wis it stertit oan a Wedinsday, A mean nothin ever sterts oan a Wedinsday kis it's the day afore pey day an A'm ey skint. Mibby git a buckshee pint roon the *Anchor* bit that's aboot it.

(from a short story 'Nice to be nice' by the Scots writer James Kelman)

⇨ (See DIALOGUE below)

DIALOGUE

Dialogue in stories has generally been seen as more or less exempt from the various rules governing spelling and grammar, because it offers itself as an exact copy of the way a particular (imaginary) individual speaks. Usages which would be incorrect outside the protective fence of speech marks bring variety and energy to the story.

This applies to dialect:

'That's about the shape o't, 'a b'lieve,' said Jan Coggan. 'Ay, 'tis a very good family. I'd as soon be under 'em as under one here and

there. Her uncle was a very fair sort of man. Did ye know en, shepherd – a bachelor-man?'

(Thomas Hardy, Far From the Madding Crowd)

and to colloquial / slangy talk:

"That's a federal officer of some kind, most likely DEA. He moves his leg look for the bulge. You savvy bulge? Something stuck to his ankle, under his pants. His backup piece... <u>Hey</u>. Try it without looking right at him if you can."

(Elmore Leonard, Get Shorty)

Dialogue is conventionally indicated by single quotation marks around all the words actually spoken. Double quotation marks are also found, though British usage favours the single marks in novels; on the other hand, British newspaper usage tends towards double quotation marks in reported comments. American practice in fiction is to use double marks. (The second excerpt above is from an American crime novel.)

Other (less usual) ways of indicating dialogue are to employ a fresh line for each new piece of speech but no other indication that this is speech, or to introduce each bit of dialogue with a dash:

- There is too much talk about, Kit said. There is leaking.

- If there is that, Raleigh said bluntly, it will be from one that cannot keep sealed under drink what has been said in sobriety.

(Anthony Burgess, A Dead Man in Deptford)

DIFFERENT FROM / TO

There is a commonsense reason for preferring *different from* to *different to* – namely, that differences are about divergences, the way things can be separated <u>from</u> each other:

The response of the under-20s was different from the reaction of those who were older.

Different to, which is a popular usage but disliked by some, might be defended on the grounds that it is a shorthand way of saying *different (in comparison) to*, but the first version is preferable.

(*Different than* is standard in US English and sometimes found in British English.)

DISCOMFIT / DISCOMFORT

To *discomfit* (verb) is to <u>disconcert</u>:

The lecturer was discomfited to see only three people in the room.

(The associated noun is *discomfiture*.)

As a verb *discomfort* has the sense of to <u>deprive of comfort</u>, but it is more often used as a noun and generally in a physical context:

He experienced some discomfort after the operation.

There is some common ground between *discomfit* and *discomfort*, but also a distinction that is worth maintaining, as shown by this example:

We all join in the fun, because we rightly like seeing those who govern us discomfited, and we know cycling is a discomfort.

(The Times)

DISINTERESTED / UNINTERESTED

This is one of the real minor battlegrounds of English usage. It's not only purists who would say that there is a clear distinction between the two words. *Uninterested* means <u>bored by</u>, <u>not attracted to</u>:

Few newspaper readers are uninterested in the private lives of public figures, though some pretend to be.

Disinterested means <u>neutral</u>, <u>impartial</u>. Correctly, this is the sense in which it's used in these examples:

"... we officers have to be non-political – we have to be a disinterested public service."

(quoted in The Times)

...his disinterested love of literature... contributed greatly to the magazine's success.

(The Times)

But for a long time now *disinterested* has been used to mean what *uninterested* means (i.e. <u>bored by</u>), and this switch of use even gets dictionary support. Eventually the newer meaning is likely to drive out the older one. Then it will no longer be possible to be simultaneously *interested* <u>and</u> *disinterested*, as a judge or a football referee ought to be (that is, attentive to proceedings but not showing bias towards one side or the other), because it will sound like a contradiction in terms.

Correct usage demands the distinction between the two words. Plenty of people continue to observe it, as the quotations above show. It's a difference of meaning that still has a bit of life left in it.

As a noun, *disinterest* can mean both <u>impartiality</u> and <u>lack of concern with</u>. Here the balance is tilted even more sharply in favour of the second definition, although the first one is the original meaning:

...from first frame to last, Hitchcock shows cavalier disinterest in the private life of the killer ...

(Donald Spoto on Rear Window).

DISTINCT / DISTINCTIVE / DISTINGUISHED

These adjectives tend to run into each other but they have separate functions. *Distinct* means <u>standing out</u>, <u>noticeable</u>:

There's a distinct smell of gas in the kitchen.

To describe something as *distinctive* suggests that it is <u>typical of</u>, <u>characteristic</u>:

Foie gras is one of the distinctive products of south-west France.

Distinguished means <u>eminent</u>, <u>worthy of respect</u>:

After a distinguished period as Foreign Secretary, he retired to write novels.

DOUBLE NEGATIVE

The very obvious double negatives, such as:

He never said nothing *or* **She ain't been nowhere**

are always inappropriate in any kind of writing – except where someone's words are reproduced in dialogue. Such phrasing would be unacceptable too in most forms of spoken English. The logic for rejecting double negatives is that the two negatives cancel each other out, so that **He never said nothing** comes to mean **He said something**. In fact, no listener can ever have been in any doubt that a double negative is simply a reinforcement of the speaker's true meaning; double and even triple negatives were acceptable in the written English of hundreds of years ago. They are now seen, however, as the mark of the uneducated speaker.

Double negatives still creep into fairly standard speech and writing:

He hasn't a chance, not even if he tries for a hundred years.

She'd never agree, no way.

and here their function is to stress the negative component of each statement. There is a more subtle type of double negative in:

She was no longer prepared to not speak out.

He was not unhelpful when we asked for information.

In both sentences the double negatives provide a distinct shade of meaning which would disappear if they were expressed as follows and given a more 'logical' sense:

She was prepared to speak out.

He was helpful when we asked for information.

Double negatives structured along the lines of *not un-* indicate a tentativeness, an uncertainty, in the user about what's being said, and an unwillingness to commit to a positive statement.

The only kind of double negative that is better avoided (other than the obviously ungrammatical 'She ain't done nothing' type) is where the negative words are placed close together and the whole statement is likely to leave the listener or reader puzzling over what is meant:

'We cannot leave nothing happening.'

(interviewee on Radio 4)

(The speaker meant: 'We must make something happen; at the moment nothing is.' But it takes a moment to work it out.)

DOWN TO / UP TO

In one of those odd shifts of language the once-universal *up to, as in:*

It's up to the government to do something about it.

has been driven to near-extinction by *down to*:

And we felt a little fresher which is down to that area of high pressure in the North Sea.

(HTV weather forecast)

Down to combines, rather neatly, the two senses of due to / owing to and the responsibility of. When applied to people, *down to* places the task-to-be-done more firmly on their shoulders than the meeker-sounding *up to; there is even a note of aggressive obligation about* the phrase:

It's down to the individual to make his own travelling arrangements.

DRAFT / DRAUGHT

Draft as a noun is a first version of something like a plan or document, and as a verb means to produce a rough, early version:

He drafted the outline of his speech on the back of an envelope.

This kind of *draft* involves words, and its producer is a *draftsman*. By contrast, a *draughtsman* works with designs or pictures. The noun *draught* describes beer, or the air that comes through a quarter-open door.

(US English, sensibly, has only one spelling: everything is *draft*. One of the US senses of *draft* is compel [someone] to do military service, the British equivalent being 'call up'.)

DUAL / DUEL

Dual is an adjective meaning twofold: *dual* control; *dual* personality.

Duel is a noun or verb indicating an arranged fight between two individuals, usually over some abstract concern like honour rather than any tangible object.

DUE TO / OWING TO

This distinction used to be a favourite in some grammar and usage books. It is, arguably, not worth preserving, but for the record *due to* should be used only in an adjectival sense, so that it is actually qualifying a noun:

The outbreak of food-poisoning was probably due to the shellfish.

(due to qualifies 'outbreak')

It is, in traditional terms, wrong to put down *due to* when the phrase applies to a complete clause:

✘ The ferry arrived late due to the bad weather.

(Grammatically, *due to* qualifies 'ferry', but is being used to apply to the whole clause 'The ferry arrived late'. The sentence should read: **The ferry arrived late owing to the bad weather.** An alternative phrasing would be: **The late arrival of the ferry was due to the bad weather.**)

The different applications of *due to / owing* to are not observed by many people, and this is not a case where one can say that anything is lost by a technical incorrectness. The real objection to both phrases, I think, is that they sound incurably bureaucratic. *Due to* and *owing to* come straight from the station announcer's public address system or the local authority circular. Most of the time *because of* can be used, and this not only produces simpler English – **The ferry arrived late because of the bad weather** – but also avoids the problem of whether to put *due to* or *owing to*.

EATABLE / EDIBLE

If something is *edible* then it's <u>safe to eat</u>, that is, it won't poison you:

Many kinds of mushroom are not edible.

If *eatable* then it is <u>fit to eat</u>, even quite good – but the word does not convey great enthusiasm and you wouldn't use it to compliment someone on the cooking. The adjectives are used almost interchangeably:

"It's all very well trying to impose quality standards but these strawberries were perfectly edible."

(quoted in the <u>Sun</u>)

(the producer presumably wanted them to be *eatable* as well)

ECONOMIC / ECONOMICAL

Economic means <u>relating to the economy</u>, and is a term that reflects the large-scale concerns of a Chancellor of the Exchequer or a board of directors:

The Treasury today issued its economic forecast for the coming year.

Economical is an altogether more homely term, and when applied to an individual means <u>careful with money</u> (with a hint of stinginess); when used about products it suggests that the consumer is getting value for money:

This is an economical car: it averages 50 mpg.

Economical can also suggest <u>sparing, small in quantity</u> (an *economical* portion). One of the best known euphemisms of recent times was when a senior British civil servant acknowledged in court that he had been 'economical with the truth' (i.e. lied).

EFFECT

⇨ See AFFECT

E.G. / I.E.

e.g. and *i.e.* (almost always appearing in lower case, and sometimes without full stops) are abbreviations of Latin phrases which are occasionally confused.

e.g. (*exempli gratia*) introduces an <u>example</u>, one or two out of several:

American lawyers (e.g. John Grisham and Scott Turow) have written some of the most successful novels of the 1990s.

i.e. (*id est*) introduces an <u>explanation</u>, or <u>another way of putting things</u>:

Crossing the 'line' (i.e. the Equator) was once a shipboard ritual.

EGOIST / EGOTIST

There is a thin distinction between these two nouns, both of which denote the <u>self-centred individual</u>. An *egoist* is someone who systematically and selfishly puts his or her own interests first, oblivious to any other considerations, and someone who would defend his right to do so if challenged.

An *egotist* is a cruder, perhaps less successful version of the *egoist*; the *egotist* thinks a lot of himself (in both senses), talks frequently about himself, assumes others find him as wonderful as he finds himself.

EITHER

When *either* appears by itself as the subject of a sentence it takes a singular verb form since, by definition, *either* refers to one (of two):

Either of them <u>has</u> a good chance of winning.

EITHER...OR (IS / ARE)

When a singular noun or pronoun appears after *either* and *or* the following verb should also be in singular form:

Either he or you <u>has</u> to make the choice.

The verb which follows takes the form appropriate to the nearest pronoun; so:

Either he or I <u>have</u> to make the choice.

Where the nouns or pronouns are plural the verb is in agreement:

Either the strains of the journey or her earlier misfortunes <u>were</u> too much for her.

If one subject is singular and the other plural the verb agrees with the nearest, although such a construction doesn't make for a very natural sentence:

Either neighbours or a passer-by <u>was</u> the first to raise the alarm.

(but would be **Either a passer-by or neighbours <u>were</u>**...)

⇨ (See NEITHER...NOR)

ELDER / OLDER

Of these two adjectives in the comparative form (the superlatives are *eldest* and *oldest*), *older* can be used in almost any context (an *older* person, an *older* car) while *elder* is restricted to people, generally within a family framework (my *elder* sister).

Elder also has the noun sense of someone who should be looked up to, on account of years of experience, as in 'elders and betters' (though it is hard to imagine this phrase being used now without a tinge of irony.)

ELICIT / ILLICIT

The words may be confused because they sound almost identical. The verb *elicit* means to draw out:

A few careful questions elicited the real reason for her presence.

The adjective *illicit* means not allowed, unlawful. The word carries a stealthy overtone, but is less forceful than 'illegal':

... illicit [video] copies of Disney productions are swelling the coffers of drug barons ...

(Guardian)

ELISIONS

Elision (or contraction) is the term to describe the way in which words are shortened by leaving out one or more letters:

didn't

I'll

she'd

let's

won't

you're

Elisions are universally used in speech, except in the most formal situations, and the simpler examples such as **it's** or **couldn't** are generally acceptable in writing, but it is important to bear in mind both the tone which the writer is aiming at and the intended audience.

Consider these newspaper passages (contractions underlined):

It's another blow for the stunning Dane's self-confidence just weeks after INXS rocker Michael Hutchence ditched her for another OLDER woman – Paula Yates. Green-eyed Helena was heart-broken as she'd hoped to marry heart-throb Hutchence.

(Daily Star)

We visit historical sites, go to places where so many things about life haven't changed a bit – ox-ploughs biting up the earth, say, or women in long black dresses -that we vaguely sense we've gone back in time.

We look at buildings where the order of the stones <u>hasn't</u> changed much in 400 or 900 years.

(Independent on Sunday)

... the battle of economic ideas before the next election will not be over the lush political pastures of taxes, interest rates and public spending; instead it will cover such barren and unfamiliar territory as business training levies, export credit guarantees ...

(The Times)

Changing the first two segments by ironing out the contractions seems a very small business: **It is another blow...she had hoped to marry**, in the first; **have not changed a bit... we have gone back... has not changed much**, in the second. But doing this would alter the tone or 'feel' of what the writers intended. The first is a piece of showbiz gossip. It may be interesting, but it's certainly not serious for anyone except perhaps the participants. Precise, formal English would be out of place. The second excerpt, about searching for evidence of the past in Holland, is a laid-back bit of argument in an article that combines history and travel. It's apparent from the writer's style that he's aiming for something personal, and not a stiff, academic style.

The third is a short excerpt from a *Times* editorial. If you try the reverse exercise, and shorten the expressions here, substituting **won't be over** for **will not be over**, or **it'll cover such barren and unfamiliar territory** for **it will...**, then some of the weight and dignity of the article start to trickle away. And if the writer had done what some <u>speakers</u> would do with the first line, and elided 'election' and 'will' – ... the battle of economic ideas before the next election'll not be over... – he or she would really have been in breach of the conventions of formality which govern serious prose, since this is an elision which appears only in speech or in reported dialogue. A greater informality might not matter too much as far as newspaper editorials are concerned, but what if Churchill had said in one of his famous World War II speeches: **'we'll fight them in the fields and in the streets, we'll fight them in the hills...'** ? A very damp rallying-cry, and infinitely less impressive when written down.

Some people consider contractions out of place in almost any kind of writing except the most informal, but there is no justification for this view. Many elisions like **they've** or **didn't** have been acceptable in written English prose for hundreds of years, even if other, more elaborate ones involving two apostrophes placed closely together – **couldn't've, I'd've** – cannot really be used in any but the most easy-going prose. This isn't an area where 'rules' apply, but widespread use of the contracted forms of phrases will give a relaxed air to what a writer has to say, almost irrespective of subject matter, while avoiding contractions altogether produces a 'correct' prose which invites itself to be taken seriously. It is less a question, then, of subject matter than of the note which the writer wants to strike. A job application letter which started: 'I'm just dropping you a line to ask whether you've still got any vacancies...', would probably get the casual response which its casual tone invites.

⇨ (See also COULD OF; LETTERS)

ELLIPTICAL DOTS...

One of the functions of this small string of dots (conventionally, only three of them) is to indicate where words have been omitted in a quotation. If the following sentence:

Learners will have to pass a theory exam on all aspects of motoring, including effect on the environment, before taking the practical test.

(Daily Star)

was to lose its central section in quotation it would be written:

Learners will have to pass a theory exam... before taking the practical test.

Elliptical dots suggest that a relatively small number of words has been excluded from the quotation, and shouldn't be used to indicate that, say, a lengthy paragraph has been jettisoned with only an opening and a closing phrase left behind – although blurb writers have a tendency to do exactly this! The fundamental sense of a sentence should remain when material is omitted using elliptical dots; their function is not to distort the original meaning of a quoted passage but to cut out a section which isn't relevant to the present writer's purpose.

Elliptical dots are also used to indicate where letters have been omitted from individual words. In practice this is confined to those terms which some newspapers don't print in full for fear of offending readers (asterisks and dashes serves the same function):

"If c....s were orange he'd be a f.....g Jaffa."

(Bernard Manning, quoted in the Independent)

Decorum is observed. The writer or editor knows what the words are; the reader knows what the words are too. But one has chosen not to push them in the face of the other.

Dots are also used to show that a statement or story isn't complete, that it has been interrupted, or simply tailed off, or that a period of waiting has started. (Technically, these are 'suspension points' rather than 'elliptical dots'.)

To be continued...

at the end of an episode in a serial, provides the classic example.

... sending 1,300 posse members into South Phoenix, to lie in wait for graffiti vandals and other vermin ...

(Independent on Sunday)

(Here the first row of [elliptical] dots are mine, and show that the excerpt is part of a longer sentence whose beginning I haven't quoted. The second row of dots, or suspension points, are the author's and indicate that time will pass before the next event in the narrative occurs.)

Dots are occasionally used as a stylistic device to slow the flow of a passage. In the following example they are the equivalent of an indrawn breath:

And they're marching to... *disaster*, **because the viaduct ends in a sheer drop.**

(Independent on Sunday)

ELUSIVE

⇨ See ALLUSIVE

EMEND

⇨ See AMEND

EMINENT / IMMINENT / IMMANENT

Eminent, an adjective, means <u>conspicuous</u>, <u>distinguished</u>, and is usually applied to people:

The company requires an eminent chairman to raise its public profile.

Imminent, an adjective, means <u>about to happen</u>; it is applied to events, almost always in a threatening context.

The raised voices and tense expressions showed an argument was imminent.

The two words should not be confused:

✗✗My views would hardly receive so much attention from such imminent people if I had not made the original mistake.

(William Rees-Mogg, The Times)

Immanent is a rare adjective with a specialist religious / philosophical meaning of <u>pervading</u>, <u>inherent</u>.

(The noun forms are *eminence*, *imminence* and *immanence*, respectively.)

EMPATHY / SYMPATHY

Both nouns are to do with <u>feeling</u>, but have slightly different applications. *Empathy* is <u>imaginative identification</u> <u>with someone else</u> and his or her situation, whether that situation is a good or bad one:

During the training session one of the counsellors played the part of an abused child with real empathy.

Sympathy also involves the attempt to see things from the perspective of another person and carries the additional sense of <u>compassion</u>.

As we'd only recently been burgled ourselves I had sympathy for the neighbours when their house was broken into.

(The related verbs are *empathise* and *sympathise*.)

ENDEMIC / EPIDEMIC

Endemic, an adjective, means <u>widely found in a certain group or district</u>, and although it may refer to a disease it can extend to other areas:

Poverty and prostitution were endemic in Victorian London.

Epidemic is a noun or adjective describing an <u>outbreak</u> – usually of a disease (though one could talk of 'an *epidemic* of panic'). A characteristic of an *epidemic* is that is relatively short-lived, unlike something *endemic*, which is there for good:

The world was ravaged by an epidemic of Spanish 'flu after the First World War.

ENORMITY / ENORMOUSNESS

Enormity is <u>extreme wickedness</u> or a <u>crime of extreme wickedness</u>:
...the enormity of Hitler's crimes had been exposed...

(The Times)

In recent years the word has also been used in the sense of <u>vastness</u> (ie, *enormousness*), though some would say this usage is incorrect. This sense, relating purely to size, may eventually oust the other one meaning 'outrage', but at present there is still something odd about a phrase like:

✗ The enormity of the universe ...

(Guardian)

The preference for *enormity*, when what is really meant is *enormousness*, may have something to do with the cumbersome quality of the second word, and there are occasions when the two senses do seem to run together:

Yossarian choked on his toast and eggs at the enormity of his error...

(Joseph Heller, Catch-22)

ENQUIRY / INQUIRY

Inquiry should be used for an official investigation:
– **the Greater Manchester Police Inquiry – the Scott Inquiry – 'helping with inquiries'**

This version of the word may also be used in the less threatening sense of merely <u>asking for information</u>:

He said yesterday that he had received numerous inquiries in response to the advertisement ...

(The Times)

but the general preference is to use the other spelling in such contexts **(enquiries welcomed)**.

[Most dictionaries simply list 'enquiry' as a variant spelling of 'inquiry'. American usage favours 'inquiry'.]

ENSURE

⇨ See ASSURE

ENVIOUS / JEALOUS

It is difficult to draw a precise line between these two words. Yet, while many people probably wouldn't object to being thought of as *jealous*, at least occasionally, no one likes to be termed *envious*, since it suggests someone who is <u>small-minded and resentful of other people's success</u>. In personal relationships, *jealous* is the appropriate expression. And although one wouldn't want to be called *envious*, other adjectival forms of the noun *envy* – such as *envied*, *enviable* – carry quite a positive weight. To talk of someone's being in *enviable* circumstances, health, etc., doesn't indicate that the speaker is consumed with bitter hatred. This kind of *envy* might even demonstrate good taste:

... the theatre, one of our most enterprising, successful and internationally envied industries ...

(The Times)

EQUABLE / EQUITABLE

The adjective *equable* means <u>even, without extremes</u>:

He had such an equable temperament that it was impossible to pick a quarrel or an argument with him.

Equitable means <u>just, following the principles of fairness</u>:

An equitable division of the property made the divorce less difficult than it might have been.

ESPECIAL / SPECIAL

The adjectives *especial* and *special*, and the adverb forms (*especially*, *specially*), are used almost interchangeably although there is a distinction between them. *Especial* and *especially*, meaning <u>principal, very much</u>, intensify whatever word they are linked with: an *especial* friend; an *especially* happy day.

Special is very often used in the sense of *especial* (a *special* friend, etc.) but it carries the additional sense of <u>specific</u> or <u>confined to a particular subject</u>:

I had a special reason for wanting to see you today.

Special can be a noun: today's *specials* (on a menu); or an adjective: *special* circumstances.

(*Especial* is an adjective only, and should not be used in the sense of 'specific' shown above.)

EUPHEMISM

A *euphemism* is an alternative way of saying something which the speaker or writer is afraid might cause offence if expressed more directly or bluntly. *Euphemisms* cluster round those areas of life which are embarrassing or threatening: death, sex, bodily functions.

Such expressions include:

sleep with / be intimate with / have relations with;

spend a penny / pay a visit / wash one's hands (as in 'Do you want to wash your hands?');

pass away / pass over to the other side / sleep (when meaning die / be dead)

It would be almost impossible to avoid some trace of *euphemism* in our language, however much we might pride ourselves on being plain speakers. Even statements such as 'The car's run out of petrol' could be seen as a self-defensive and euphemistic way of deflecting blame onto the inanimate car and away from oneself: an alternative to confessing 'I was too stupid / forgetful / preoccupied to remember to get some petrol.' And it's a rare neighbour who, when asking to 'borrow' some milk / sugar, actually intends to return it. 'Borrow' is here a *euphemism* for 'have'.

Where a *euphemistic* expression is intended to protect another's feelings (or even one's own), and springs from a genuine sense of tact, it shows sensitivity – rather than being the cop-out which some people consider the *euphemism* to be. Where, however, the *euphemism* is intended to hide something then it is more deserving of Bernard Levin's stern judgement: 'Every euphemism is a lie'.

As employed by groups, whether governments, businesses, institutions, *euphemisms* are almost always designed to conceal or, at least, to make something sound more attractive. For example (*euphemism* first, 'translation' second):

gender confirmation surgery = sex change operation

standard class = second class

savings = financial cuts

disadvantaged / underprivileged = poor

incentive = bribe

downsizing = sacking people

shrinkage = losses through shoplifting (or **alternative shopping**, as seen from the other side of the counter)

pre-emptive strike = attack without warning

collateral damage = destruction brought to civilians outside bomb target area

A few euphemisms operate as a kind of code understood by reader and writer but not spelled out in clear English for legal reasons, or simply because they have acquired joke status. In this way, 'tired and emotional' is used for drunk (or intoxicated, an alternative, mild euphemism); and 'confirmed bachelor' for homosexual (or the more euphemistic 'gay'). For the satirical magazine *Private Eye*, 'Ugandan discussions' are shorthand (or perhaps longhand) for sex. Expressing something in a euphemistic way can sometimes be merely comic, whether intentionally:

> **As he shuffles towards life's departure lounge, he is naturally anxious to make his peace with his family.**
>
> *(Daily Express)*

or unintentionally:

> **A diver had gone missing, and a shredded diving suit found. "We prefer to call most of these incidents 'interactions' rather than attacks," said a [Florida] spokesman on behalf of the sharks, "because they are cases of mistaken identity when a shark is going after a meal..."**
>
> *(Independent)*

EXAGGERATION

Exaggeration is natural in speech, where speakers vie with each other to go over the top in approval or disapproval of another person, a song, an experience, etc. It's less usual in the cooler, more detached conditions of written English, although there's still a tendency to intensify responses in less formal contexts: according to some newspapers, people are 'staggered', 'knocked sideways', 'gobsmacked', or 'shaken to the core', when they are probably no more than mildly surprised.

Certain areas seem to encourage exaggeration. Business writing is one.

Here is a true arena for the survival of the fittest. Macho activity moves from the predatory:

> **Mr Smith said the group was still hunting for a suitable acquisition.**
>
> *(The Times)*

to the massacre (in which, one might think, it would be good to be overlooked):

> **But as often happens, some good companies have been overlooked in the bloodbath.**
>
> *(Independent on Sunday)*

to wholesale annihilation:

> **The nuclear option is to put it into receivership.**
>
> *(The Times)*

There's nothing wrong with this kind of writing (though it gives an interesting insight into the chest-beating self-image of the City – or at least of the financial correspondents). The trouble is that reaching for the extreme parallel, right up to nuclear war, can look a little absurd. And, in some cases, a touch tasteless. Here the writer compares a bad film to the Nazi war crime trials:

> **Eddie Murphy's Harlem Nights stands as Exhibit A in the Nuremberg of movie crimes perpetrated by actors who have no talent as directors.**
>
> *(Guardian)*

⇨ (See also UNDERSTATEMENT)

EXALTED / EXULTANT

Exalted (adjective) means high, dignified:

> **Despite his exalted position, the President never lost touch with his roots.**

Exultant (adjective) means triumphant:

> **They were exultant after the 5 – 0 victory.**

(The associated verbs are *exalt* and *exult*, while the noun forms are *exaltation* and *exultation*.)

EXCEED

⇨ See ACCEDE

EXCEPT

⇨ See ACCEPT

EXCEPTIONAL / EXCEPTIONABLE

Both of these adjectives derive from the noun *exception* which has the double meaning of something excluded and an objection. *Exceptional* means outstanding, excluded from the normal run of things:

> **That summer was exceptional for its low rainfall.**

Exceptionable means objectionable (i.e. describes something to which *exception could be taken):*

> **It wasn't the plan but his aggressive way of explaining it that the committee found exceptionable.**

Because the two words are often confused, with *exceptionable* used (wrongly) in the sense of *exceptional*, there may be an ambiguity in sentences such as:

> **It took an exceptionable time for the luggage to arrive.**

EXCLAMATIONS

Much more common (and acceptable) in speech than in writing, words such as 'What!' or 'Hey!' form a separate category as parts of speech. As expressions of alarm, delight, revulsion and so on, they are usually spontaneous and, in themselves, have no meaning. Exclamations are sometimes called interjections, a term that covers such usages as 'well', 'er', 'um', 'oh', 'hurrah'. An interjection is a 'throwing between', something that breaks up the flow of words. Expressions like 'well' or 'um', particularly in response to a question, are ways of buying time, expressing uncertainty, etc., and are therefore out of place in formal prose, where the writer is supposed to have done his thinking and his hesitating before committing himself to disc or paper. Would you trust a newspaper editorial which began 'Er, um...'?

Nevertheless, the use of such words is increasingly frequent in relatively informal or humorous writing. 'Hey' is especially popular:

> **It takes a real man to get into a clinch with Sharon Stone and not check under the bed for ice-picks, but – hey! – Sylvester Stallone is up to the task in The Specialist.**
>
> *(The Times)*
>
> **And it seems that the only people more bored and disillusioned with Radiohead than myself were, um, Radiohead.**
>
> *(The Times)*
>
> **...a little-known album by someone called Billy Joel. Whoa! Slow down there!**
>
> *(Independent)*
>
> **Everyone knows that Margaret Thatcher has been, well, stinting, in her admiration of John Major and his colleagues.**
>
> *(Guardian)*

'Er' too has been turned into a joke interjection, popularised by *Private Eye*, and, like one of the uses of inverted commas, casts an ironic or comic light on its context:

> **We all, of course, remember her in great films such as Carry On Up Your Knickers and... er ...**
>
> **The consultants? Er, Coopers & Lybrand.**
>
> *(both Private Eye)*
>
> **So next year Easter will be on... Er**
>
> *(Independent on Sunday)*

Some writers use exclamations / interjections as part of their stock in trade. The following is a selection from a single article by Bernard Levin in *The Times*:

> **Oh, *what* if everybody did it?**
>
> **Ah, the angels weep...**
>
> **(hurrah! may there be many more ignorings!)**

Use of archaic exclamations such as 'forsooth!' or 'gadzooks!' is better avoided altogether; they sound ridiculous even when the user means them ironically.

EXCLAMATION MARK

When placed at the end of a sentence, as it generally is, the exclamation mark serves the same function as a full stop. It should be used where the context demands it:

'**Oh no!**'

'**Help!**'

'****** off!**'

'**Fire!**'

'**O horror, horror, horror! Tongue nor heart**
Cannot conceive nor name thee!'

(Shakespeare, Macbeth)

Where a piece of speech is accompanied by a word like 'shouted', 'screamed', 'barked', the exclamation mark will naturally take its place at the end of the words actually spoken; if the identity of the speaker and the verb come after the quotation no capital letter is used for the first word following the exclamation mark (since the sentence isn't actually finished):

"**But you haven't been on yet!**" **she expostulated.**

(Independent)

No capital letter is used after an exclamation mark if it is placed in the middle of a sentence, for example to signify a noise or an oath. However, the phrase affected by the exclamation mark should be placed between commas or dashes:

For all our frankness and agony-columns, that shade still falls, clack!,
every time.

(Libby Purves, The Times)

Exclamation marks are subject to the law of diminishing returns. The more often they are used the less urgent they become. They can pep up a piece of prose, but their overuse is likely to leave the reader wondering what all the fuss was about:

What fun these rich folk had, to be sure! And then Bond remembered.
But of course! It was Christmas Eve! God rest ye merry gentlemen, let
nothing ye dismay! Bond's skis hissed an accompaniment as he
zigzagged fast down the beautiful snow slope. White Christmas! Well,
he'd certainly got himself that!

(Ian Fleming, On Her Majesty's Secret Service)

Exclamation marks can also be used to register a writer's surprise at what he is reporting. This usage has something ironic or humorous about it:

Peter Walker rejects the idea that he was ill and puts his condition
down to too many chocolate biscuits!

(John Campbell, Edward Heath)

The Suit! The classical suit of impeccable pedigree! Is such a thing worn today?

(Guardian)

Smart media opinion was that only one member of her Cabinet was first-rate – Lord Carrington!

(Guardian)

Exclamation marks are best avoided in formal writing (e.g. a CV or an application letter), given that both drama and humour are usually missing from such contexts.

EXHAUSTED / EXHAUSTIVE

Exhaustive means very thorough:

She gave an exhaustive account of her one-woman trip by canoe up the Amazon.

Exhausted is just very tired:

That one-woman canoe trip really left her exhausted.

EXHORT / EXTORT

To *exhort* is to encourage, to urge:

Henry V exhorted his men before Agincourt.

To *extort* is to obtain something, usually money, by violence or the threat of it:

The protection gang extorted money from half the clubs in the city.

(The noun forms are, respectively, *exhortation* and *extortion*.)

EXPECT

⇨ See ANTICIPATE

EXPLICIT / IMPLICIT

These adjectives are both applied to the meaning of something but in opposite senses. *Explicit* is frank, clear:

The notice gave an explicit warning that shoplifters would be prosecuted.

(*Explicit* is also a shorthand term for frankness in language or the depiction of sex in the media. As such, it can operate as a warning [when a television announcer prefaces a film with a statement about 'explicit language'] or as an inducement to watch and listen.)

Implicit means suggested, not openly stated:

He was too polite to say so, but implicit in his manner was the idea that he would have done a better job.

(*Implicit* also carries the sense of <u>absolute, unquestioning</u>: *implicit* trust.)

FAMOUS / INFAMOUS / NOTORIOUS

If being *famous* is a desirable state, then to be *infamous* is to be <u>very well-known for something</u> <u>undesirable</u> – but the source of the infamy is likely to stimulate strong curiosity, even an obsessive interest. In other words, there's a kind of back-handed compliment in applying the term:

Jack the Ripper's infamous crimes

the Marquis de Sade's infamous novels

Notorious can be used as a straight substitute for *infamous*, but it also appears in lighter contexts:

"Oh, he's notorious for eating fifteen packets of cheese & onion and downing twenty lagers a night."

(The nouns related to the adjectives are *fame, infamy* and *notoriety*.)

FARTHER / FURTHER

Farther means the same as *further*, and is preferred by some people when physical distance is the topic:

We overtook them a few miles farther on.

The more widely used *further* could be substituted in the sentence above, and should always be the choice when the sense of <u>extra, to a greater degree</u> is required:

Inflation rose further than expected last month.

(*Further* is the variant used in expanding an argument: "Further, I would like to say...".)

FEWER / LESS

Both of these adjectival comparatives (*few / fewer*; *little / less*) indicate a smaller number or quantity. *Fewer* should be used when referring to a number of objects or people (i.e. with a plural noun):

There are fewer swimmers in the pool today.

Less should be applied to any singular item:

Health experts advise us to put less salt on our food.

It is quite usual to find *less* used with plural nouns:

✗ There are less openings for graduates in this area.

but *fewer openings* sounds better as well as being grammatically correct.

FLAIR / FLARE

Flair is a noun indicating <u>a natural ability</u> in something (a *flair* for languages), while *flare* as a verb is to <u>blaze out</u> or, as a noun, denotes <u>a sudden light</u> (generally some kind of warning signal). It's this second spelling – *flares* – that describes the trousers of the 1970s, the decade when taste took a back seat.

When the two words are confused it's usually because the second is used in error for the first:

✗✗ He had a particular flare for recruiting new members...

> *(The Times)*

[and another flare for when he was lost at sea?]

FLAMMABLE / INFLAMMABLE

Both adjectives mean the same, <u>capable of</u> being (easily) <u>set on fire</u>. The story goes that flammable was 'invented' because the *in-* prefix on *inflammable* looked like a negative (along the lines of 'visible / invisible') and suggested that the thing described could <u>not</u> be set on fire. Is there any recorded case of someone dropping a match on an item labelled *inflammable* and being surprised when it went up in flames? Nevertheless, *flammable* is the preferred alternative.

FLAUNT / FLOUT

To *flaunt* is <u>to make a public exhibition of</u>, <u>to show off</u>:

> **The glamour girl of the Fifties flaunted her 36D-23-35 figure in low-cut tops...**
>
> *(Sun)*

To *flout* is <u>to treat something with contempt</u>; it's generally used when laws, rules, conventions are being disregarded – in a very public way:

> **"They flouted the law just to get publicity."**
>
> *(Advertising Standards Association spokesman, quoted in the Sun)*

The two terms are sometimes confused:

✗✗ It [the Commonwealth] has drawn up a formal mechanism for suspending and even expelling nations that flaunt its values.

> *(The Times)*

FLOUNDER / FOUNDER

These two verbs, very similar in sound and meaning, are often confused. To *flounder* is to <u>struggle</u>, to <u>stumble</u>:

> **Without his notes he was floundering for something to say.**

To *founder* means to <u>fall in ruins</u>, to <u>sink</u>, and might be seen as the next (and last) stage after *floundering*. The verb is sometimes applied to horses, who might *founder* on the home straight, but most often to ships and, in a figurative sense, to people's schemes:

It was a great plan but it foundered because he couldn't persuade the others to share his vision.

FOREIGN WORDS & PHRASES

English is the lingua franca of scientists, of air pilots and traffic controllers around the world, of students hitchhiking around Europe, and of dropouts meditating in India or Nepal.

(Robert Claiborne, Englis̲h̲ ̲–̲ ̲I̲t̲s̲ ̲L̲i̲f̲e̲ ̲a̲n̲d̲ ̲T̲i̲m̲e̲s̲)

Perhaps it is the fact that English is so widely spoken and accepted around the world which accounts for the rich hoard of words from other languages which we find in it. English speakers tend to be tolerant, even welcoming, in their attitude to foreign imports.In France, by contrast, the body of scholars called the French Academy is concerned with maintaining the purity of the language and tries officially to discourage such imports as 'le parking' or 'le weekend'. The author, quoted above, of a book about English uses an old Italian phrase ('lingua franca') to describe the universality of the language. English speakers get everywhere – are everywhere – and, by choice or by necessity, have gathered fragments of other languages which have then worked their way into the body of English.

Names of foods (hors d'oeuvres, spaghetti, frankfurter, goulash), Latin phrases (ad lib, ad nauseam, ad infinitum, etc.), more exotic imports (kiosk – from Turkish; veranda – from Hindi) – all can be used naturally and without apology. No 'translation' is necessary because all of these terms have embedded themselves thoroughly in English. And no word is too antique to make itself at home. The Greek expression 'hubris' (meaning 'arrogance', the ambition to take on god-like powers) has become something of a vogue word recently:

It [Denver Airport] is also, critics insist, one of the largest white elephants ever built, a massive monument to hubris.

The first casualty of Talk Radio UK... is the hubristically-named programme S̲u̲c̲c̲e̲s̲s̲.

(both T̲h̲e̲ ̲T̲i̲m̲e̲s̲)

And ever since the Queen used a Latin tag to describe a year she had not enjoyed the same phrase has surfaced in unlikely places:

It has been another Annus Horribilis for the royals.

(S̲u̲n̲)

The kinds of words mentioned earlier (pizza, kiosk) have been completely anglicised. They don't really feel foreign any longer. But others retain the flavour of their sources. They don't sound English – yet. There are two reasons for using them in speech or writing. One is to show off, although this often doesn't amount to more than a tongue-in-cheek pomposity. The other, more respectable, reason is that such foreign words and phrases capture or suggest a concept for which there is no exact equivalent in English. They do a job for which our own language lacks the precise tools.

> ...the KGB's two principal *betes noires* during the 1980s, Ronald Reagan and Margaret Thatcher...
>
> *(The Times)*

> At one time it was *de rigueur* for any new office block development to include parking spaces for employees...
>
> *(The Times)*

> Having the hump is one of Lindi's favourite expressions. She uses it all the time, apparently unaware of the *double Entendre*.
>
> *(Independent)*

> ...Tarantino, golden boy or enfant terrible of the movie world, depending on your point of view...
>
> *(Guardian)*

Of these examples *double entendre* might be rendered as 'double meaning' but would lose the tinge of sexual suggestiveness which the phrase always carries in French. The others have strands of meaning requiring lengthy unravelling, and even then would probably not be adequately explained. *De rigueur*, for instance, conveys the idea that something is both necessary *and* fashionable.

For some words there isn't an English equivalent at all:

> A degree of *Schadenfreude* surrounds the grisly task of clearing up the mess.
>
> *(Independent)*

(*Schadenfreude*: a German term meaning pleasure in other people's discomfort or unhappiness)

> ...UK workers could be in danger of succumbing to Japanese-style *karoshi* – death from overwork.
>
> *(The Times)*

It is possible to use foreign phrases in a self-mocking, tongue-in-cheek style, as when the writer of this article recounts a de luxe (French import) night out at the theatre:

> ...it will make queueing at the box office seem pretty *infra dig* in future... And when it was time to go we still did not have to mingle with *hoi polloi*.
>
> *(David Lister, Independent)*

Half a century ago, in an essay called 'Politics and the English Language' George Orwell advised: 'Never use a foreign phrase, a scientific word or a jargon word if you can think of an everyday English equivalent'. The advice is good, but rigorous. A frantic search to find good old Anglo-Saxon alternatives every time a piece of jargon or a foreign term crops up would be a waste of time and energy. But the use of imports from other languages can sometimes seem to be nothing more than an elevated form of showing off:

> **The lifestyle that commuting offers him, and *ergo* the reason for his commuting is plain to see... and many offices could be based *ex urbis*...**
>
> *(The Times)*

(Why not 'therefore' and 'outside the town'?)

And although 'faux pas' is familiar enough it's a little hard to see why the writer of the following had to go to the Japanese when he was searching for a word that means 'tidal wave':

> **But the *faux pas* has triggered a *tsunami* of homophobia.**
>
> *(Observer)*

ITALICISING FOREIGN WORDS

In printing, foreign words are generally italicised. The equivalent in handwriting is underlining. Dictionaries provide guidance on whether a particular term should be italicised. As a general rule, the more familiar a term the less it needs to be singled out in this way. Words and expressions such as 'autoroute', 'trattoria', 'tour de force', 'ad hoc', 'ad nauseam' are fairly well embedded in English. Others (e.g. *tour d'horizon, ultra vires*) are relatively obscure, and should be italicised. There is a category of half-familiar terms – son et lumiere, hors d'oeuvres – which the writer can choose to leave unmarked. The markings and accents of the word should be preserved: doppelgänger; cliché; château. Care should be taken over the few words which, if not distinguished by accents and / or by italicisation, could be read as English terms: e.g. pâté requires its accents; without them it might just be mistaken for 'pate', the (admittedly dated) English expression for head. The Latin term *pace* (meaning 'by the leave of' – a courteous way of introducing a disagreement with another's opinion) needs to be italicised or underlined to avoid confusion with the much more familar English 'pace'.

FORTUITOUS / FORTUNATE

Fortuitous means <u>occurring by chance</u>:

> **They were just talking about him when he made a fortuitous appearance at the door.**

Fortunate is <u>lucky</u>:

> **Considering the offence he was fortunate to receive only a suspended sentence.**

FULL STOP

A full stop marks the end of a sentence. The main errors in placing full stops involve (fairly obviously) leaving them out where they are required or including them where they are not.

TOO FEW FULL STOPS

Leaving out full stops where they are required obscures the writer's meaning or suggests confused thinking. In the following examples an extra full stop is needed, or at the least a stronger piece of punctuation than a comma:

✗ Not all banks are the same, it really is worth considering making a change.

(First Direct advertisement)

(full stop after **the same**, or a semi-colon or a dash)

✗ No one likes paying taxes, but most of us have to, please take some time out to read this ...

(Council Tax leaflet)

(new sentence should have been started with '**please...**')

✗✗ Get a life, with a caravan by the sea at Orchards, its just a 'stones throw' from London.

(advertisement)

(a sentence that requires major surgery, but among other things that are wrong the comma after **Orchards** should be replaced by a full stop or a colon; **its** should read **it's**, of course.)

✗✗ 95 has been an extremely busy year for our client NT or new technology has kept its existing staff on their toes, they have been learning about new products; becoming more and more experienced giving them a broad range of technical skills.

(IT recruitment advertisement)

(A complete mess. Should be a full stop after **our client**, and another after **their toes**. The semi-colon should be replaced with a comma, and a comma inserted after **more experienced**, and 'gaining' substituted for **giving them**.)

COMMAS USED IN PLACE OF FULL STOPS

A confident writer can use commas where full stops or other punctuation would have been grammatically more correct. This may be because what follows the comma is very closely connected to what comes before:

A trailer truck was rumbling past, it filled the booth with noise and Diesel exhaust.

(Ed McBain, Goldilocks)

(Compare this with the example from the *First Direct* advertisement above. There the *it* doesn't relate back to anything, but here *it* plainly refers to the truck.)

Commas can be used when a string of clauses sets up a rhythm and particularly where there is a single subject to the sentence:

I was exhausted, I was numb, I didn't know what I was feeling or thinking.

(Ed McBain)

Sometimes commas are used to separate a piece of prose because the writer wants to give an easy, conversational tone to the material, where fact and opinion jostle against each other:

The last thing I wanted was to throw Della, things are tough enough, the whole world is lying in wait to wrong-foot her, but I needed to set out my stall, so I began anecdotally by telling her that, driving up, I had been listening to the car radio and heard John Redwood described as "vulcan", so what will we find if we look up "vulcan" in her spanking new dictionary?

(Alan Coren, The Times)

To write like this you need control over your material.

TOO MANY FULL STOPS

The opposite mistake to omitting full stops is to include them where they are not required at all or where other, lighter punctuation would have been adequate. This is usually a 'mistake' in the technical sense, because it's a device much used by advertisers and others who want to make points in a punchy way.

Also included with the PCTV is the Microsoft works package. Designed to give order to the untidiest of minds. It allows you to tackle all manner of word-processing and financial tasks. And produce presentation-quality charts and illustrations. Effortlessly.

(computer advertisement)

The last four sentences here could have been written more correctly as a single sentence, with only one comma required (**Designed... minds, it allows you...**). But doing this would have robbed the commentary of its bite-sized, easily digestible gobbets of information.

A sentence is still a sentence, however, and while a single word (such as **Effortlessly** in the example above) may make sense in context it will not usually compose a grammatical sentence in itself. Tacking a full stop onto the end of a cluster of words won't necessarily make for a sentence; in the example below a rash of full stops makes nonsense of the piece:

Coming into the room. He saw a man he half recognised sitting on the sofa. And smoking a cigarette. His first thought was to ask him. What the hell he was doing. But something about the man's manner. Stopped him. It was almost as if. It was not his room. But one that belonged. To the man on the sofa.

⇨ (See also SENTENCE)

FULL STOP IN ABBREVIATIONS

The tendency is to omit full stops. In particular, if the abbreviated word ends with the same final letter as when it is spelled out in full the convention is to drop the stop. This covers some very common abbreviations like **Mrs**, **Mr**, **Dr**, **St**, **Rd**, which appear more often in their shortened form than in full. Where the word is cut off halfway through or earlier – **Prof.**, **max.**, **Co.**, **Sat.**, etc. – the full stop is more often retained, and is useful in indicating that only a portion of the word appears.

With acronyms like **NATO** or **AIDS** full stops are not used. The tendency is to avoid them also in abbreviations that are made up of initial letters even where those letters do not spell anything which can be pronounced:

... an extension of qualified majority voting (QMV) ...

... The National Association of Head Teachers (NAHT)...

And it is also increasingly usual to find the full stop omitted in names (although strictly correct usage would retain them):

W H / W.H. Auden

H G / H.G. Wells

P D / P.D. James

⇨ (See ABBREVIATIONS)

FURTHER

⇨ See FARTHER

GAMBIT / GAMUT

A *gambit* is an opening move, originally in chess (where the term applied to the deliberate sacrifice of a piece in order to gain an advantage of position). Now the term is extended to any thought-out manoeuvre in a game, negotiation, and so on.

The team's intimidating gambit was to utter a series of war cries before each match.

(An *opening gambit* is a tautology or repetition – all *gambits* are opening ones, by definition.)

Gamut means range, the full spectrum:

Sir Edward Lutyens's fluent drawings run the full gamut, from monumental projects to cosy, intimate spaces.

(Independent)

The first word is often found, incorrectly, where the second is meant:

✗✗ '... a whole range of things, a whole gambit of ideas...'

(Rugby Union commentator, Radio 4)

GENDER: he / she / they? & other problems

An interesting issue of usage – and also one which is pretty well impossible to resolve satisfactorily – concerns the appropriateness of **he** and **his** as standard pronouns when the gender of the relevant noun is unspecified. The custom, until recently, has been to use the masculine pronoun throughout, as here:

> **It is only through education that the individual has the chance to achieve his humanity...**
>
> *(The Times)*

> **The reader will recognise the voice of truth when he hears it. If he does not, so much the worse for him.**
>
> *(Iris Murdoch, The Black Prince)*

or when the feminist writer Angela Carter talks about how '**the text constantly reminds the reader of his own troubling self...**'.

The application of these statements isn't confined to men, of course. Women readers are included under the he / his umbrella. Then why not write **to achieve her humanity** or **the voice of truth when she hears it** or **reminds the reader of her own troubling self**?

Habit is the answer. Convention. A few years' persistent replacing of **he** and **his** with **she** and **her** in English prose would quickly make the latter look 'normal' – if enough people did it. As things stand, many readers (of either sex) probably experience a slight hiccup if they come across sentences such as:

> **Any viewer will find herself gripped at once. A Prime Minister ought to know her own mind.**

It's impossible to avoid the feeling that the writer is making a point here – which they probably are – and the point (that an unidentified, 'unsexed' individual may just as well be a woman as a man) can overshadow the ostensible content of the sentence if the reader is distracted by it.

In speech, and relatively informal writing, the issue can be sidestepped by using the colloquial **they / their**:

> **'I want everyone to tell me their story.'**
>
> *(William Trevor, quoted in The Times)*

> **For everyone who ever thought the person they loved was out of their reach.**
>
> *(film advertisement)*

> **But a great key to the psychology of the individual is not what they believe to be happening but the gross, overt effects of their actions, both for themselves and for those around them.**
>
> *(Independent)*

Another way round the problem is to use the **he or she** formula:

> **The right-minded assistant professor in the post-Vietnam era imposes**

his or her politically correct attitudes upon the literature of the past.

(David Lehman, Signs of the Times)

...will the Amis of 2001 have his (or her) novels published on the Internet?

(Guardian)

This works well enough for a sentence or so, but gets cumbersome if the sentence requires frequent use of the pronoun and the writer is dutifully coupling **she / her** to every **he / his**.

Another ingenious tactic is to combine the two pronouns:

(S)he will have responsibility for the organisation, direction and management of the Faculty ...

(academic advertisement)

This unisex pronoun (more usually s / he) works only on paper; it can't be said aloud and retain its double meaning. Similarly with other forms of the double pronoun; they cannot be said, and the objection might be made that a word which isn't pronounceable is an over-ingenious answer to a problem:

... the material that an author selects for treatment or discards as insignificant tells us much about hrmself, hrs milieu and hrs expected public...

(Kenneth Dover, Marginal Comment)

If you want to avoid using **they** and **their**, which is perfectly good for most types of writing except the formal, then the **he / she** formula is a good substitute. The other options are to stick to the rather dated formula of employing **he** full time, something which many people find unacceptable, or to rephrase the sentence altogether. Applying this last solution to the very first example quoted above would make it read **It is only through education that individuals have the chance to achieve their humanity...** A further option is to avoid personalising the sentence altogether, e.g. **It is only through education that the individual has the chance to achieve humanity**. Similarly, in my earlier sentence beginning **It's impossible to avoid the feeling that the writer is making a point here – which they probably are...**, where the gender of the writer is subsumed under the informal 'they', the last part might be rephrased – **which is probably the case...**

SPOKESPEOPLE

Where the sex of the spokesperson or chairperson, etc is known it is correct to make a sexual distinction by saying 'spokeswoman', 'chairman', etc., although it is not uncommon even now to find the suffix -man applied to women, as in 'Lady Howe, Chairman of the Broadcasting Standards Council'.

There's been a certain amount of fun at the expense of '-person' as a suffix – along the lines of **She was wearing her Walkperson** – because it sounds slightly awkward, and (more likely) because its use appears to be another bow in the direction of Political Correctness.

Certainly it can be used with deliberate humour:

> **Two Mafia hitpersons (Jack Nicholson and Kathleen Turner) fall for
> one another ...**
>
> *(Independent on Sunday)*

but in more obvious expressions like 'chairperson', 'layperson', frequent use
will eventually stifle the objections which, in most cases, have a hint of sexism
about them.

ACTOR / ACTRESS?

The tendency is to avoid words that designate the sex of the person carrying
out a particular job. Therefore, 'actor' describes a man or a woman, as do
'author', 'poet', 'sculptor' '(bus) conductor'. The feminine forms of some of
these terms (authoress, poetess) not only sound dated but have a faint air of
amateurism, as if the woman were merely dabbling in the activity.

In those few areas, mostly the service industries, where men and women
have always been on a more equal footing, the feminine form may be retained:
waiter / waitress; steward / stewardess; headmaster / headmistress. 'Hostess',
however, has clip-joint associations, while 'host' can be used of either sex.

GET

Over-use of *get*, either in the sense of <u>obtain</u> or as part of expressions such as
get through, *get at*, is usually held up as a stylistic error. A run of *'gets'* will
sound monotonous or awkward:

> **I got up, got dressed, and had almost got through the front door when
> I got delayed by the phone.**

In a sense, *get* is just too useful. Although for the sake of variety alternative
expressions should be found sometimes, certainly when one is writing or
speaking in formal contexts, there is no need to go on a witch-hunt after *got*.
The word has a brisk, semi-colloquial vigour which is valuable. All four *'gots'*
might be omitted or replaced in the example above:

> **I rose, dressed, and was almost through the front door when I was
> delayed by the phone.**

but there is a difference between the slightly dated **I rose** and **I got up**, and this
is a case where the more familiar, natural expression may be preferable.
Similarly, **dressed** sounds more formal than **got dressed**. It all depends what
tone the writer is aiming for.

⇨ (See also NICE)

GOBBLEDEGOOK & OTHER NONSENSE

Gobbledegook is jargon or, simply, nonsense, or – at its least bad – language
which is struggling with complicated concepts, and losing the battle. It's
language with ambition. Sometimes it is bureaucratic, sometimes specialist.

Although pressure groups such as the Plain English Campaign have sharpened the clarity of official documents some legal or contractual language can still cause the eyes to glaze over:

> ... where retirement takes place after Normal Retirement Age but not later than the Member's 70th birthday, paragraph 1(b)(ii) and (iii) shall not apply, and if retirement is later than the attainment of that age, the said paragraphs shall apply as if the Member's 70th birthday had been specified in the rules as his Normal Retirement Age, so as not to treat as service after Normal Retirement Age any service before the Member reaches the age of 70 ...

> *(pension document)*

Sometimes such writing is merely pretentious, not because it is aiming high and grasping at subtleties, but because its main purpose is to impose its own look-at-me cleverness on the reader, who is almost always going to have to go back and ask: 'What did that mean?':

> But for Burroughs, Gysin was a hierophant, the decocter of the auguries. When they plunged into the noumenal together, Burroughs found there ample confirmation of all the magical suppositions he had always had.

> *(Will Self, Guardian)*

There is also a type of writing which seems to make sense on the surface but where the writer has obviously been on autopilot:

> Forcing Microsoft to unbundle now would have been just about feasible; closing the door after the horse has bolted is going to be virtually impossible.

> *(Independent)*

Of course, bolting the door after the horse has bolted is not difficult but very easy – and also completely pointless.

⇨ (See also JARGON)

GRAND / GRANDIOSE

The difference between these two adjectives is that *grand* should be applied to something which is authentically splendid while *grandiose* suggests that what is described is somehow inflated or false. A *grand* building is large and very imposing, a *grand* scheme is ambitious and conceived on a great scale. *Grandiose* ideas, by contrast, are hollow; they sound good but will never amount to anything.

(*Grand* also has some currency as a colloquial term of approval, like 'brilliant', 'great', etc., although the term is a little dated now.)

HANGED / HUNG

Everything should be *hung*. Pictures on walls, coats on racks, meat in the butcher's; even people can hang when they are clinging on to something:

He hung from the window-sill by his fingertips.

The single exception is in the context of capital punishment, when the individual is *hanged*. The wrong word is frequently used:

✘ **'He [John Brown] was, caught, tried and hung.'**

    (Wish You Were Here, ITV)

✘ **He was arrested immediately, found guilty of "moral insanity" and hung.**

    (Big Issue)

HISTORIC / HISTORICAL

Historical is an adjective meaning <u>relating to history</u>, and attaching it to a noun says nothing about the significance of that noun. It's a 'neutral' word:

Recent historical research has tended to investigate the lives of 'ordinary' people rather than those of rulers and generals.

Historic indicates that the event, person, battle, etc so described was <u>important, history-making</u>:

The first testing of an atomic bomb, at Los Alamos in July 1945, was an historic moment for mankind.

HOARD / HORDE

Hoard is a <u>mass</u> of something valuable such as gold or money:

Rumours of a hoard of Nazi treasure at the bottom of the lake circulated for many years.

Horde describes a <u>large number</u>:

There were hordes of people in Oxford street for the sales.

The first word is wrongly used here instead of the second:

✘✘ **... someone who can fight the hungry hoards of other people who are going to apply for this job!**

    (recruitment advertisement)

HONORARY / HONOURABLE

Honorary (adjective) is applied to offices or titles held without the possessor's having to perform services to retain them – an *honorary* degree is awarded because of the eminence of the recipient, rather than because he or she has studied at that particular university or for that particular subject. *Honorary* also describes posts that are not paid: the *honorary* secretary of a society holds his or her post without any financial reward.

Honourable (adjective) means <u>deserving honour</u>:

He had an honourable career in public life, untouched by any hint of scandal.

HOPEFULLY

One of the 'misuses' of language that gets quite a few people's blood boiling. The older (and, if you like, proper) meaning of *hopefully* is <u>with hope</u>:

From the shelter of the pavilion the umpire gazed hopefully at the clearing sky.

But a much more common use of *hopefully* is as a kind of shorthand for <u>it is to be hoped that</u>:

This dispassionate approach... hopefully leads to them being able to step outside the cycle and break it.

(Independent on Sunday)

Hopefully – for Richey's sake – we will never see him again...

(The Times)

This usage is so widespread – and, it has to be said, so useful – that any expectation that the tide will be turned and people revert to applying *hopefully* in its original sense is hopelessly unrealistic.

An ambiguity may very occasionally arise with a statement like:

Hopefully she'll be starting work next week.

where it is possible that the adverb describes her attitude (she will be full of hope) rather than the speaker's optimistic expectation (it is to be hoped that...). Although the newer sense has largely driven out the old, some do object to this later application of *hopefully* and some dictionaries bracket it as (informal / colloqial).

⇨ (See also THANKFULLY)

HUMAN / HUMANE

As an adjective *human* is generally a simple descriptive term (as in 'human being'). But *humane* carries strong overtones of approval; *humane* treatment is <u>kind and considerate</u>, the right thing. The following example uses both adjectives:

...reforming Quaker Samuel Tuke began a campaign against the York Asylum which treated the mentally ill in the traditional way – as less than human. Tuke set up the rival York Retreat founded on new, humane Quaker ideals.

(The Times)

⇨ (See INHUMAN / INHUMANE)

HUNG

⇨ See HANGED

HYPHEN

To hyphenate or not to hyphenate? The question opens up one of the trickier areas of English usage. In some cases, hyphenation is necessary for the sake of clarity; in others, hyphenation is an option, and depends on a variety of factors ranging from publishers' house styles to personal preference to other sorts of convention. Dictionaries give guidance on whether particular word groups are to be hyphenated or not, but there is something of a gap between the advice and current usage. The tendency now is to reduce hyphenation, either by leaving it out altogether or by running together words that were formerly kept at arm's length by the hyphen, The hyphen is more likely to be retained with adjectives than it is with nouns and verbs.

Using a hyphen indicates that the words joined together form an entity with a particular meaning distinct from either word taken in isolation:

Grey-green

Bitter-sweet

Do-it-yourself

Tragi-comedy

Jack-in-the-box

Co-driver

Off-load

Hitch-hike

Under-use

STANDARD PREFIXES

Some prefixes don't require hyphenation: **bifocal**; **transcontinental**; **inconsiderate**; **uncommunicative**; **interrelated.** Others should include the hyphen: **ante-room**; **post-operative**; **ex-husband.** Some others take a hyphen according to the age and familiarity of the term:

minibus *but* **mini-golf**

midwinter *but* **mid-Seventies**

multicoloured *but* **multi-purpose**

semicircle *but* **semi-invalid**

(the doubling of the i's in the last example is the principal reason for inserting the hyphen in a word that would otherwise read 'semiinvalid'.)

COMPOUND ADJECTIVES

A hyphen should join compound adjectives, that is, groups of two or more words used adjectivally and where each word is closely related to the other(s):

London-based

Same-sex

Anglo-American

ever-growing

one-night (stand)

...would-be-grown-up (part of us)

(*Guardian*)

COMPOUND NOUNS

Dictionary advice on the use of the hyphen in compound nouns does differ, and using the hyphen here is frequently a matter of choice. As an alternative two words can be run together – or simply allowed to stand alone:

Tail-end / tailend

Buy-out / buyout

dressing-room / dressing room

The hyphen can safely be used in most cases and must be used in some. General advice would therefore be to use the hyphen; you're unlikely to be wrong. Cases where the hyphen must be included are words beginning 'self-' (self-confidence; self-criticism); numbers from twenty-one to ninety-nine (but not one hundred, two thousand, etc.); expressions that are essentially colloquial (mum-of-three; pick-n-mix); and words that express some fairly new concept (body-swappers; make-over).

VERBS

Hyphenation is less frequent with verbs but many require it, even if it is hard to formulate guidelines:

cross-examine

co-operate

re-examine

fine-tune

double-cross

leap-frog

back-comb

freeze-dry

de-ice

pre-empt

Missing out the hyphen in a few nouns and verbs starting 're-' or 'co-' can make for momentary uncertainty if the prefix combines with the first letters of the main word, e.g. **reerect**; **coworker** (better as **re-erect**; **co-worker**). In some cases inclusion (or omission) of the hyphen will produces different word: **recreate / re-create**; **recover / re-cover**.

Verbs which include a preposition or adverb (technically called 'phrasal verbs'), such as 'break up', 'show off', 'play back', 'take over', do <u>not</u> take a hyphen.

✗✗...but Chris... isn't fretting any more after a pal managed to pick-up a dog collar.

(Daily Star)

✗✗..before he covered-over some of his best ideas.

(Independent)

✗✗We sober-up fast when the blue light flashes.

(The Times)

However, nouns derived from phrasal verbs are <u>always</u> hyphenated or even spelled as one word: break-up; show-off; playback; takeover. The difference is illustrated by:

We had to wait three quarters of an hour after we broke down on the motorway.

(phrasal verb: break down)

It was the second break-in they'd suffered that year.

(compound noun: break-in)

ADVERBS

When adverb is placed next to an adjective the hyphen is <u>not</u> used if the adverb ends '-ly':

widely known

highly praised

With adverbs that don't end in '-ly' correct usage includes the hyphen:

long-standing

well-read

much-loved

high-achieving

AMBIGUITY IF THE HYPHEN IS LEFT OUT

The growing tendency is to omit the hyphen: a newspaper TV guide produced these examples for a single evening: **sci fi thriller; sharp edged city drama;**

steamy home counties drama. Leaving out the hyphen does not usually hamper understanding, even if correctness indicates that there should be one in these adjectival phrases. But ambiguity, often comic, can follow sometimes if the hyphen is left out. In the last example above it is the drama that is 'steamy' rather than than the home (it should have read **steamy home-counties drama**). The ambiguity is stronger in these examples:

✖ **Clarke Gable is a rubber plantation owner...**

   (The Times)

(should be **rubber-plantation**)

The phrase... despite improved rear leg room... occurred in a motoring article in the <u>Sun</u>. Without the hyphen which should be placed between 'leg' and 'room' (**...despite improved rear leg-room...**), the apparent meaning was that the car offered more space for your animals, or anyone else in your family who possessed rear legs.

   In this *Guardian* quotation it isn't a matter of a bad-tempered test but of a procedure in a court of law:

... children still have to be available for cross examination...

Care needs to be taken over 'cross' in other contexts as well:

That includes threesomes, filthy foursomes and even cross dressing.

   (Sun)

(This suggests that angry dressing took place; perhaps it was something to do with the filthy temper of the foursomes.)

While in this:

...you are therefore quite at liberty to go and have an extra marital affair

   (Independent on Sunday)

it's not <u>another</u> marital affair which is on offer, but an **extra-marital** one.

   Where a word makes the common element for two hyphenated terms, it is correct to repeat the hyphen:

Table- or lap-dancing has become a lucrative craze in the US and Canada.

   (Independent on Sunday)

and incorrect to use only one hyphen:

✖ **Adam Dalgliesh is an introspective wine and poetry-loving graduate...**

   (Guardian)

(The hyphen missing here after 'wine' is required to make the link with 'loving' which is the common element for both 'wine' and 'poetry'.)

WORD-BREAKS

When using hyphens to make a word-break at the end of a line the convention is that the word should be split up by syllables:

infiltra-tions; indepen-dence; Brit-ish; pro-cess; obvi-ous; na-ture

The unnatural way to break the above, for example, would be:

infilt-rations; ind-ependence; Bri-tish, etc.

No single syllable word should be broken (**sho-uld** would be wrong; **bro-ken** would be all right), and a single letter should never be left hanging over to the following line. It is also the convention to avoid breaking proper names even when of two or more syllables (e.g., Thom-as, Di-ana).

Newspapers occasionally throw up word divisions that give a humorous or momentarily misleading sense to a line:

...displaying the leg-

ends of saints...

  (The Times)

...prides herself on being able to give

an on-the-spot character anal-

ysis of every man.

  (Sun)

Brian Mawhinney, the Secre-

tary of State for Transport, is

trapped by his own party's dog-

ma...

  (Independent on Sunday)

I.E.

  ⇨ See E.G.

ILLICIT

  ⇨ See ELICIT

ILLUSION

  ⇨ See ALLUSION

IMAGINARY / IMAGINATIVE

Imaginary means <u>having no basis in reality,</u> <u>illusory:</u>

  Ruritania is the imaginary country of *The Prisoner of Zenda*.

Imaginative means <u>showing imagination</u> in a creative sense:

Using only a couple of chairs the group staged an imaginative reconstruction of the trial.

IMMANENT / IMMINENT

⇨ See EMINENT

IMPLICIT

⇨ See EXPLICIT

IMPLY / INFER

Properly used, these verbs have a complementary quality. To *imply* something is to hint or suggest it without its being openly stated:

Mr Karadzic will not be feeling as triumphant as his propaganda implies.

(Independent)

To *infer* is to draw conclusions from the evidence, and suggests skill at understanding hints and working out implications:

Gossip columnists began to infer from Evelyn's disappear-ances that she was engaging in reckless liaisons.

(E L Doctorow, Ragtime)

In this way one person will *infer* what another has *implied*, or (in noun terms) *inferences* will be drawn from *implications*, something Dr Watson was unable to do, according to Sherlock Holmes:

"You fail, however, to reason from what you see. You are too timid in drawing your inferences."

(Conan Doyle, The Blue Carbuncle)

Infer is sometimes used as though it meant *imply* – as in:

✘ **"I don't like your tone of voice. What are you inferring?".**

This usage gets some dictionary support, but it is wrong by the standards of correct English.

INDIGNITY / INDIGNATION

Indignity is something you endure, a humiliation:

The prisoner suffered the indignity of a body search.

while *indignation* is what you feel about it afterwards, a sense of justified anger. *Indignation* can be expressed on behalf of others and the injustice they have received as well as being felt for one's own sake:

The chairman reacted with indignation to the suggestion that he was personally profiting from the scheme.

(The adjective relating to *indignation* is *indignant*, while the adjective most nearly linked with *indignity is undignified*)

INDUSTRIAL / INDUSTRIOUS

Industrial is used of objects, places, processes, etc. and means <u>connected with industry or the manufacture</u> of goods, while *industrious*, used of people, and sometimes animals, means <u>hard-working</u>.

INFAMOUS

   ⇨ See FAMOUS

INFERIOR

   ⇨ See SUPERIOR

INFLAMMABLE

   ⇨ See FLAMMABLE

INGENIOUS / INGENUOUS

Ingenious means <u>clever</u>, particularly in the context of finding solutions for problems or thinking up new methods:

Car manufacturers have spent millions devising ingenious ways to protect their cars against salt water and other elements.

   (advertisement)

Ingenuous means <u>simple</u> – usually too much so, as it's not innocence so much as gullibility that is suggested:

Only a really ingenuous person would believe everything that he was told.

This adjective is more frequently found in its negative form: *disingenuous*. This indicates a <u>devious</u> person, plan, remark which is masked by the pretence of straighforwardness:

"... and to wear such an attention-getting accessory [as sunglasses] under the guise of wishing to deflect notice seemed disingenuous... "

   (quoted in The Times)

INHUMAN / INHUMANE

Both adjectives convey strong condemnation, and many people use them interchangeably. However, there is a distinction between them. *Inhuman*, meaning <u>brutal</u>, <u>barbarous</u>, is the harsher of the two, and appears in the context of people's behaviour towards each other, with the implication of being less than, not worthy of, a human being:

Memorial services recalled the inhuman treatment of concentration camp inmates by the Nazis.

Inhumane has the sense of cruel, lacking in qualties of kindness and sympathy. It can be used about the way individuals or animals are treated:

Protesters claimed that the veal calves were transported in cramped and inhumane conditions.

⇨ (See HUMAN / HUMANE)

INQUIRY

⇨ See ENQUIRY

INSURE

⇨ See ASSURE

IN TO / INTO

Distinguishing between these two sometimes causes problems. *In* when followed by *to* is an adverb:

He jumped in to get cool.

(*in* qualifies *jumped*)

Into is a preposition:

The Intercity train pulled into Paddington.

IRONY / SARCASM

Irony is a complex, almost indefinable concept. Very broadly speaking, *irony* concerns itself with the gap between the way things are and the way they seem to be or are spoken about. It may not be detected by the participants in a situation, and is often more apparent to the outsider. *Sarcasm*, by contrast, is both easily identified and easily used, even by children. There is some overlap between the two terms but *sarcasm* is a very junior, rather crass member of the *irony* family. If it is sometimes more effective than *irony* it is simply because it is more direct; the scornful tone of voice which wraps up a *sarcastic* remark will almost invariably be picked up by the listener. *Sarcasm* is usually spoken, and consists in simply turning upside down what you really mean: "Thanks for coming on time" to a latecomer; "Nice tie" to someone whose taste you hate. Tone of voice instantly conveys that the opposite meaning is intended. *Sarcasm* is very plainly intended to hurt, and there is a sort of playful cruelty to it even when *sarcastic* remarks are traded among friends.

   Irony falls into all sorts of categories from the obvious to the very subtle, from *verbal irony* to *irony of situation*. In Shakespeare's *Macbeth* it is *ironic* when King Duncan of Scotland rides up to Macbeth's castle full of praise for its beauty and the kindness of his host and hostess, since the audience already knows that Macbeth and Lady Macbeth intend to kill him. It is *ironic* if a fire-station burns down while the crew are out on a false alarm; if a police station is burgled; if a solicitor who has always insisted to his clients on the importance of making a will then dies without leaving a will himself. There is a dark, occasionally very bitter dimension to the word: *irony* rarely produces nice results – or if the result is right then it comes at the wrong time. The word is widely used, and should be restricted to those contexts where there is <u>a</u> <u>genuine and usually uncomfortable turn of events, often one that recoils on</u> <u>their creator</u>:

> **But perhaps the greatest irony of the Ed Wood story is the fact that, having never wanted anything to do with him while he was alive, Hollywood has now embraced him.**
>
> *(Independent on Sunday)*

> **"There is a powerful irony about a situation in which soldiers go to try to keep the peace and then find they cannot defend themselves properly as they try to keep it."**
>
> *(quoted in the Independent)*

The term *ironic* is better avoided when discussing situations that are merely surprising, as in: 'It was ironic that we won our final game after being defeated all season.' No *irony* is involved here.

(*Ironic* and *ironical* are both adjectival forms; the adverb *ironically* is formed from the latter.)

ITS / IT'S

Its and *it's* are frequently confused. The usual mistake is to put in an apostrophe where it is not required. *It's* is the contracted or shortened form of *it is* (*It's* a warm day). *Its*, without an apostrophe, is the possessive form of the pronoun *it* (The cat flicked *its* tail).

All of the following should read *its*, with no apostrophe:

✗✗ **The cider that lives up to it's name.**
> *(Scrumpy Jack advertisement)*

✗✗ **... unlike common-or garden spring mattresses which will sag with age latex will hold it's shape ...**
> *(Dunlopillo advertisement)*

✗✗ **Unlike other films on this event, Kasdan and Costner's gives the gunfight it's factual 30 seconds.**
> *(Independent)*

✗✗ ... Real Wives, the first magazine of it's type...

    (Guardian)

✗✗ Brings it's own rewards

    (swimming pool advertisement)

Getting it wrong the other way round (i.e. leaving out the apostrophe when it should be included) is less usual but still found:

✗✗ ...Arnold Schwarzenegger finds his memory has been erased – so its off to Mars in the hope of piecing together his past.

    (Independent)

✗✗ Staff without windows say they do not know whether its dark outside, if its raining, sunny, hot or cold ...

    (Sun)

If uncertain over which form to use, try substituting the full length *it is* in the sentence. As long as the phrase or sentence still makes sense (*It is* a warm day), then you can safely use the contracted form of the two words (*It's*..). If, however, the sentence does not make sense (the cat flicked *it is* tail), then you are using the possessive form of *it* and must not include the apostrophe: write *its*. The following gets both spellings right in the right places:

But to its followers, it's the old story of demonising black subculture before exploiting its commercial fallout.

    (Guardian)

JARGON

Jargon is specialised language that originates from a particular group, usually a professional one. Thus doctors have a *jargon* that is particular to them, as do lawyers, etc. *Jargon* serves a useful purpose within a group when it enables its members to communicate more quickly as they talk about procedures, tools or concepts that wouldn't mean much to the outsider. *Jargon* also has the psychological effect of binding members of a group together and keeping outsiders in their place (i.e. outside). In this it has something in common with slang. Quite often jargon spills over into the world outside, and specialist language takes on a wider range of meaning; for example, from film / video we have terms like 'fast-forward', 'slow-motion', 'freeze-frame', 'flashback', 'rough cut', and so on. From psychoanalysis, expressions like 'inferiority complex', 'paranoid', 'manic depressive', 'schizophrenic' have passed into general currency.

    Jargon should be used when dealing with the appropriate audience, one that knows what you're talking about (here the subject is computers):

Compaq and Intel have already demonstrated the first continuous-media server hardware based on this Tiger technology.

This has been designed to provide a cheaper way of delivering video-on-demand by using standard PC components and asynchronous transfer mode switches as part of the delivery mechanism.

(Independent)

A passage like this will be understood by those who are familiar with the terminology. Outsiders presumably wouldn't be reading it in the first place, or would quickly stop if they were.

Jargon in inappropriate contexts can sometimes confuse or sound pretentious, and the writer or speaker who wants to communicate with his or her audience (rather than just impress them) will avoid it:

...women on the dealing floor [of the City] are "dimensionalised along a continuum of sexual availability". She means that they are put into categories...

(Independent on Sunday)

'...a role model of the civilised interface parents expect of their children...'

(speaker on Radio 4)

⇨ (See also BUZZWORDS, SLANG)

JEALOUS

⇨ See ENVIOUS

JUDICIAL / JUDICIOUS

Both of these adjectives are connected with judgement, the first in a professional way and the second in an 'amateur' sense. *Judicial* means to do with a court of law:

He looked at 59 courts over 5 years to examine judicial discharges ...

(The Times)

Judicious means showing good sense, with a hint of caution:

Asked about the Prime Minister's chances of surviving the vote, the Home Secretary gave a judicious reply.

KIND OF, SORT OF

The use of *kind of* or *sort of* as in:

He was feeling kind of unhappy about the situation.

We sort of hoped you would ring.

should be restricted to speech or very informal writing. The phrases have a slight blunting or blurring effect which is perfectly acceptable in speech when a tentative note is needed; in more formal contexts it is better to substitute 'rather', 'fairly', 'quite'.

LAY / LIE

These two verbs are very frequently confused in written and spoken English.

To *lay* is to <u>put down</u> and is a transitive verb (i.e. one which generally takes an object):

Lay your sleeping head, my love ...

(first line of W. H. Auden poem)

To *lie* is to <u>be at rest on a horizontal surface</u> and is an intransitive verb (one which does not take a direct object):

He told the dog to lie down at once.

Confusion mostly arises from the fact that the past tense of *lie* is *lay*:

The dog lay down and went to sleep straightaway.

while the past tense of *lay* is *laid*:

They laid the picnic food out on the rug.

The past participle form (ie, that used after 'has' or 'had') is *lain* for *lie*:

The farmhouse has lain empty for almost two years now.

and *laid* for *lay*:

Thousands of mines had been laid in the course of the war.

Mistakes like those in the following examples are quite frequent:

✗✗ The coffin had laid in the chapel overnight...

(Independent)

(should be **The coffin had lain...** because after 'has' or 'had' lie *changes to* lain*)*

✗✗ Take a rug to lay on and a sheet to shield you from prying eyes.

(Sun)

(should be **a rug to lie on** – unless you're a chicken contemplating the production of eggs.)

To *lie* in the sense of to <u>not tell the truth</u> takes a different (and regular) past tense / past participle:

They lied in claiming they were elsewhere at the time.

LESS

⇨ See FEWER

LETTER WRITING

The difference between personal and official letter-writing provides a good illustration of the gap between formal and informal English usage. Whenever we speak or write we make calculations about the 'audience' our words are meant for, and adjust our choice of words and style of speech accordingly.

These calculations are frequently unconscious, and go back to when we first learned to talk in different ways to friends, teachers, parents, and realised that some ways of saying things would go down well with one group but not with another. The different registers of English are most markedly shown in the gap between slang and formal speech or writing. This isn't to suggest that there is something artificial or fake about formal English while slang is spontaneous and natural. In fact, there is often a calculated element in the deployment of slang or colloquial English.The choice about which register to use is a basic tool in the effective use of the language.

WHAT TO SAY

Anybody writing off in pursuit of a job application is likely to want to present him or herself in the most positive light. Language will be on its best behaviour. What, then, would be the effect of opening a letter like the one below?

> Hi! Thought I'd drop you a line about you giving me a job in your company, maybe. I've always wanted to make money in financial services and someone told me your lot were the business. And I saw this ad about how you only look for the best and the brightest, so I thought to myself, that's me! Only joking. My girlfriend said for me to go for it too.
>
> I expect you'd like to know the kind of things I like doing. Well, travelling for one and just generally bumming around. Last year me and my girlfriend went to Turkey and that was quite interesting. I've got qualifications, GCSEs and A levels and all that, so I can't see any problems in the intelligence area.
>
> OK, don't think there's much else to say as of this moment, and you've probably had enough of me rabbiting on anyway. So if you don't want to miss "the opportunity of a lifetime" and take on a guy who'll work hard and play hard if the price is right, then just give us a bell. The number's at the top of the page. Looking forward to getting this sorted.
>
>   All the best
>
>
> PS Thursdays and Fridays are good times to get hold of me. The rest of the week's a bit dodgy since I'm out and about doing stuff. My girlfriend will take a message if she's in. OK?
>
>   Cheers

A letter which would be more favourably received would be one that was clear and accurate and stuck to the subject, as well as one that avoided colloquialisms (such as 'OK'). These considerations in fact apply to the writing of all good, formal English.

```
     I am writing in response to your advertisement
of 15th September in The Times, and would like to
apply for one of trainee posts available in your
company. I am a recent graduate from the
University of Sussex, where I gained a 2:1 in
French and Economics. My CV is enclosed.
     The high reputation of your company and your
extensive interests in Europe, particularly
France, have been addtional attractions for me.
     I would be pleased to supply any further
information you might need and look forward to
hearing from you.
                                   Yours faithfully
```

ADDRESS

The sender's address goes at the top of the letter in the right hand corner or, more often on headed notepaper, across the top of the page.

In formal letters the name and address of the recipient are placed on the left hand side, below the sender's address and above the opening of the letter itself. This is a useful convention, particularly if the letter is being sent to an office or organization, because it shows clearly whom the letter is directed at.

The date should be included on any letter except very informal ones.

Convention about what follows *Dear* is changing slightly. *Sir* or *Madam* is fairly formal and the tendency is to use the recipient's surname with the appropriate title: *Dear Mr / Mrs / Miss / Ms Smith.* The full name is also used: *Dear Michael Smith.*

SIGNING OFF

Until recently there was a distinction between 'Yours faithfully' (sometimes 'Yours truly'), to be used at the end of letters written to people whom the writer did not know, and 'Yours sincerely', used in a context that was still formal but where the writer knew the recipient. 'Yours sincerely' is found almost everywhere now, and life is slightly simpler. The old distinction was based more on etiquette and 'form' than on a useful difference. However, someone who initiates a correspondence which closes with 'Yours faithfully' may like to be answered in the same way. 'With best wishes' or some variant is quite often found, and is a warmer alternative to (or may accompany) 'yours sincerely'. Any other and more intimate messages to close a letter are entirely between the sender and the recipient.

LICENCE / LICENSE

The noun form is *licence*:

TV licence

driver's licence

off-licence

while the verb is *license*:

"Are you licensed to drive this vehicle?"

⇨ (see also ADVICE / ADVISE; DEVICE / DEVISE; PRACTICE / PRACTISE; PROPHECY / PROPHECY)

LIE

⇨ See LAY

LIKE

The widespread use of *like* in sentences such as:

So I'm like standing there thinking 'Who is this?'

is a usage restricted to speech, and should not appear in written English, even the most informal.

⇨ (See also RIGHT)

LIKE / AS IF

⇨ See AS IF / LIKE

LITERAL

Something which is described as *literal* is something which exists or has occurred precisely as stated. The words that are used are meant in their primary sense, without any metaphorical application:

The spacecraft travelled over the far side of the moon.

A *metaphorical*, as opposed to *literal*, use of a similar phrase would be:

They were over the moon at the last-minute goal.

Here the writer makes the distinction between *literal* and *metaphorical*:

City-dwellers – you stink. Not metaphorically, I fear, but literally. In your millions, you smell appalling.

(Independent)

Literal and *literally* are often used, wrongly, as intensifiers, a way of emphasising to the listener or reader that the writer really means his or her words:

The book provides such a realistic picture of the Middle Ages that you can literally smell the stench of the narrow streets.

(only if the pages have been impregnated with some chemical)

> **'... giving Prime Minister's questions where he literally wiped the floor** [with his opponents]'
>
> *(Jeffrey Archer, BBC1)*

(only if the Prime Minister was using his opponents as substitutes for mops)

LO(A)TH / LOATHE

Lo(a)th – with or without the middle *a* – is an adjective indicating reluctance, being <u>unwilling</u>:

> **I'd be loath to get involved in their quarrels.**

Loathe is a verb meaning to <u>regard with disgust</u>:

> **She loathed his insinuating, flattering manner.**

(Although the definition suggests distaste amounting to revulsion, the word is often used to signify a mild aversion, as in **I loathe the taste of beetroot.**)

LOSE / LOOSE

As verbs these words are occasionally confused. To <u>mislay</u> has one 'o' (*lose*); to <u>set free</u> has two (*loose*)

LOOSE / LOOSEN

To *loose* is to <u>set free, cast off</u>:

> **We loosed the dinghy from its moorings.**

To *loosen* is to <u>make looser</u>, to <u>untighten,</u> either literally or figuratively:

> **A few drinks certainly loosened his tongue.**

LUXURIANT / LUXURIOUS

Both adjectives derive from *luxury* but have distinct meanings. *Luxuriant* describes anything which is <u>produced in abundant quantities</u>; its use is generally restricted to natural growth (hair, foliage, etc.):

> **... *luxuriant trees and bushes of white poinsettia filled the* campus ...**
>
> *(Independent on Sunday)*

Luxurious conveys notions <u>of great comfort</u>, expense and (often) flashiness:

> **The house has the self-made man's stamp of being rather too meticulously luxurious to rank as a true grandee's residence.**
>
> *(The Times)*

MACHO / MANLY / MANNISH

Manly, which means <u>brave, fitting for a man</u>, isn't used much now, perhaps because it has stiff-upper-lip, Victorian overtones. *Masculine* would be the modern equivalent. *Macho* is a rough (in both senses) contemporary equivalent but carries a suggestion of swaggering masculinity which the Victorians would certainly not have approved of:

> **The International Conference was a fairly macho negotiating forum, with a great deal of banging of fists on tables and ripe language ...**
>
> *(Independent)*

(*macho* should be pronounced 'matcho', not 'macko'; the noun is *machismo*.)

Mannish can be applied to women who are considered insufficiently 'feminine' – and for this reason it may sometimes be code for 'lesbian', rather as 'confirmed bachelor' is for a male homosexual (used by journalists wanting to avoid writs for libel).

⇨ (see also CHILDISH / CHILDLIKE, WOMANLY / WOMANISH)

MAJORITY / MANY / MUCH

Majority is a noun meaning the greater number:

> **The majority of the people favoured the death penalty.**

Majority should not be used to mean 'the larger part' of something which cannot be not split up into individual elements:

✗✗I was on tenterhooks for the majority of the play.

(this should read 'for most / the greater part of')

The adjective *much* is used with a singular noun: **It's too much trouble.** It should not be used with a plural or collective noun:

✗✗There's too much people on the bus.

The adjective *many* is used with a plural:

> **In the Old Testament, Job was afflicted with many troubles.**

MASTERFUL / MASTERLY

The adjective *masterly* means highly skilled, brilliantly accomplished, and is most often used when a performance of some kind is being praised:

> **Many will never forget his masterly appearances on TV, smoking the pipe that became his symbol ...**
>
> *(The Times)*

Masterful is sometimes used to mean the same thing, but it carries overtones of bullying, of aggressive assertion, and describes the kind of man who flexes his muscles in a frock-coat on the cover of a bodice-ripper romance:

> **A masterful individual, he wouldn't tolerate opposition.**

It's not always clear whether a writer means it in this second sense (of domineering) or is using it as a synonym for the more complimentary *masterly*, although when applied to performances, films, etc., rather than people, the sense is usually 'highly accomplished':

James Stewart laid his amiable all-American guy persona on the line in Hitchcock's masterful thriller-cum-psychodrama [Vertigo] ...

(Independent)

MAY / MIGHT

There is a growing tendency to use *may* in all circumstances, even where *might* would be correct.

May is the present tense form:

We think he may ring.

Might is the past tense:

We thought he might ring.

(It would be wrong to say: ✘ ✘ We thought he may ring.)

However, *might* is often used in the present tense:

He might ring.

This phrasing suggests greater doubt on the user's part than *may*.

May and *might* are used almost interchangeably when following 'have', but there is a shade of difference in absolutely correct English. *May have* indicates that a possibility remains open:

He may have rung; I haven't checked the answerphone.

Might have signifies that something is no longer possible:

He might have rung if he hadn't been unexpectedly called away.

(In addition, *might have*, used colloquially, can express disappointment or frustration: **He might have rung!**)

MEDIUM / MEDIA

Media, a collective term for means of communication such as television or newspapers, is the plural form of *medium*. As a plural it should take the appropriate verb form:

The media are influential in shaping people's opinions.

The tendency is to treat the word as singular noun (an 'it' rather than a 'they'):

So why does the media disagree?

(Independent)

... what the media, for better or worse, has done for royalty...

(The Times)

Strictly speaking, this is incorrect, but it is apparent that *media* is on its way to becoming a collective noun which can take singular or plural as the writer wishes, particularly when (as in the examples above) the *media* is / are seen as

a single homogenous lump.
  ⇨ (See CRITERION / A; STRATUM / STRATA)

METER / METRE

A *meter* is a measuring instrument: parking *meter*; *milometer*.

Metre is the basic unit of length in the metric system (three *metres* in length). This is the spelling that is also used to describe poetic rhythm, the contrasting sounds between long and short or stressed and unstressed syllables.

(US usage has one spelling for both words: *meter*).

MILITATE / MITIGATE

These two verbs are sometimes confused. To *militate*, followed by 'against', is to work against, to operate to the disadvantage of:

Lack of qualifications militates against the chances of employment.

Mitigate has something of an opposite meaning – it is to lighten, to make less harsh (mitigating circumstances in court will reduce the sentence which the defendant would otherwise receive):

The best available instrument for mitigating poverty, Wilson decided, was central government.

  (Independent on Sunday)

MIXED METAPHORS

A mixed metaphor is a linguistic car crash. When a writer or speaker jams together two metaphorical phrases (i.e. phrases in which language is not used literally) they may blend beautifully; on the other hand they might mix as easily as, well, chalk and cheese. Mixed metaphors occur when their creator is unaware of the literal potential which lurks at the bottom of all metaphor:

These results only reflect part of the iceberg.

  (Radio 4)

(a conflation of 'part of the picture' and 'tip of the iceberg')

  '...sitting on the fence trying to bridge a virtually unbridgeable gap...'

  (quoted on News at 10, ITV)

(fence-sitting and bridge-building may not be incompatible activities but together they conjure up a funny picture)

Similarly with:

A sticking point, which had been a fly in the ointment on previous occasions when settlement was close...

  (The Times)

Its laid back approach to the problem may be coming home to roost.

  (Independent)

During the past 24 hours the veil of secrecy has cracked

(Channel 4 News)

This is a para-nationalist front in full cry with a different agenda.

(Radio 4)

Major saddled with spectre of new stalking horse

(Daily Telegraph)

In the marathon they call the race for the FA Carling premiership tonight should tell us whether Manchester United have hit the wall...

(Daily Telegraph)

Will he for once have the stomach for an up-hill battle if the wheels start to fall off?

(Sun)

...a European airline industry still plagued by lame ducks that soak up tax-payers' money.

(Independent)

Metaphors can be deliberately mixed to produce something that sounds odd or arresting. This <u>may</u> be the case with the following:

He pinpoints the pointlessness of knee-jerk violence...

(The Times)

(some idea of testing reflexes with a pin is called up here)

But in this example the writer wasn't really thinking through the associations of his imagery. Talking about the food provided on the Eurostar train service, he said:

The service on Eurostar in fact bears no resemblance to that, though there have been teething problems with the catering.

Impossible not to think that they ought to provide food that isn't so tough on the teeth. Unfortunately, the writer went on in the next sentence:

Feedback from users is mainly positive ...

(Independent)

suggesting that food is provided on a sale-and-regurgitate basis.

MORAL / MORALE

Moral as an adjective means <u>connected to questions of right and wrong</u>:

"We are not going to be moral guardians and stand in judgement."

(quoted in the Sun)

As a noun it is used in the singular only in the sense of <u>lesson</u> (the moral of a story).

Morale describes the <u>spirit of a group</u> such as a body of soldiers, a football team, etc.:

Morale plunged when all home leave was cancelled for the next three months.

(*Moral* is pronounced with the stress on the first syllable; *morale* rhymes with 'pal'.)

MUCH

⇨ See MAJORITY

NEITHER

When *neither* appears by itself as the subject of a sentence or clause it takes a singular verb form since, by definition, it refers to one thing:

He said neither of them <u>was</u> there.

⇨ (See EITHER)

NEITHER...NOR

Neither should be followed by *nor* (and not *or*):

The couple in front of me neither rock, shimmy, shake nor even tap their toes; nor do they applaud ...

(Independent)

Sometimes, when a string of negative possibilities follows the initial *neither...nor*, the writer slips back into using *or*:

✗ **It is neither respectful of its local architectural heritage nor interesting or brave or hopeful with any kind of futurism.**

(The Times)

but *nor* should be used throughout.

NEITHER...NOR (IS / ARE)

Neither... nor, when followed by a pronoun or noun in the singular, takes a verb form in the singular:

Neither the winner nor the runner-up <u>was</u> present to receive the prize.

With nouns or pronouns in the plural the verb is in agreement:

Neither his threats nor his pleas <u>were</u> having the slightest effect.

Where there is a mixture of singular and plural, the verb agrees with the word nearest to it:

Neither my neighbours nor the vicar <u>was</u> able to persuade me to change my mind.

(but **Neither the vicar nor my neighbours <u>were</u>...**)

⇨ (See EITHER...OR)

NICE

Nice is heard in speech much more often than it is seen on the page, probably because its unsatisfactoriness as a term of pleasure or approval has been drummed into people since school. Find a more precise word! But it's actually one of those convenient English words of endorsement, an understated counterpart to terms like 'brilliant' or 'terrific', and as such has a perfectly legitimate place in the language. Nevertheless, it should be used sparingly on paper, and probably not at all in formal contexts – if only because someone is likely to pick you up on it and say, 'What exactly do you mean by nice?'

(*Nice* has an older meaning of <u>precise</u>, <u>calling for subtle distinction</u>:

It's a nice point as to which of them is more to blame.)

⇨ (See GET)

NONE

None, where it plainly means <u>not one</u>, takes a singular verb form since, by definition, it refers to somebody or something in the singular:

None of them <u>was</u> willing to undertake this delicate task.

But *none* can also carry the sense of <u>no persons</u>, and the sentence above could be rephrased:

None <u>were</u> willing to undertake this delicate task.

Because *none* is generally used in conjunction with a plural noun or pronoun (*none* of...) there is a natural tendency to use the plural verb form:

✘ **None of the contestants have any prior knowledge of the questions.**

<u>*(The Times)*</u>

and, while it might be claimed that the sentence would read more accurately as **None of the contestants has...**, the combination of *none* with a verb in the plural receives some very active support from various venerable authorities like Sir Ernest Gowers and Eric Partridge and Bill Bryson. So, don't worry. Whether you use a verb in the singular or the plural with *none* you will be right.

NOTORIOUS

⇨ See FAMOUS

NOUNS

A *noun* is a name – of a person, place, object, feeling, idea, and so on. Details of the various noun categories will be found in the Glossary. Most 'problems' with nouns arise from the way they relate to the verbs connected to them.

NOUN / VERB AGREEMENT

A noun in the singular must be followed by a verb which agrees with it in number, i.e. is in the singular form too:

The house <u>was</u> on the market for several months...

while plural subjects require appropriate agreement from the verb:

... and few other properties in the area <u>were</u> selling.

SINGULAR & PLURAL

Two singular subjects linked by 'and' require a plural verb:

He and I are both hoping to attend.

Where the 'and' joins words that can be regarded as a single unit the singular form of the verb is used:

A short back and sides was what the barber gave me.

Fish and chips is a staple part of the British diet.

Figures in measurements, distances and quantities are treated as a singular subject if they work as unit:

Twenty-two miles is a fair distance!

A hundred pounds wasn't quite enough to get by on.

SEPARATION OF SUBJECT AND VERB

When the subject of a verb is cut off by a long intervening stretch from that verb, it's easy enough to make mistakes, and use a plural verb form with a singular noun:

✗✗ ... off-licences are complaining that boot-legging by people illegally reselling imports from France are threatening to put them out of business.

> *(The Times)*

(should be **boot-legging... is threatening** – but the plural nouns 'off-licences', 'people' and 'imports' probably jogged the writer into repeating the 'are' which had already appeared).

This mistake is a two-way street, and singular verb forms are often tied to plural subjects. In both the following **is** ought to be **are**:

✗✗ ... the sudden onset of creaking walls and window frames and a slight swaying sensation if you are sitting in a high-rise building is no longer unnerving ...

> *(The Times)*

(two singular subjects, 'onset' and 'sensation', joined by 'and' = one plural)

✗✗ The jungles of sugar-cane, a traditional hide-out for outlaws since the

18th century, is impassable to the security forces chasing the gunmen.

(The Independent)

Where there is little or no gap between the subject and the verb there is correspondingly less reason for going wrong:

✗✗ The mistrust and suspicion that poisons relations between France and the United States ...

(The Times)

(should be... poison...)

✗✗ Perched on top was Sir Nicholas's spectacles, his pocket diary, his military medal, a sporran ...

(The Independent)

(should be **Perched on top were...**)

COLLECTIVE NOUNS

Some collective nouns (government, audience, crew, team) can take singular or plural verb forms:

The Government <u>is</u> expected today to announce...

The team <u>were</u> very positive about their chances.

Common sense might suggest that if the collective noun really is thinking / feeling / acting as one then the singular verb fits better, while if there is a divided reaction the plural would be more appropriate. There are no absolute rules here, and examples will be found which don't correspond to the suggestion above:

The mob who taunted him at Clapham are long forgotten.

(The Times)

In any case, associated words (such as 'this', 'its', 'their') should be in agreement with the verb.

✗ This SW6 based company are looking for someone a bit special...

(recruitment advertisement)

(taking out the descriptive 'SW6 based' you are left with **This company...are**).

Consistency is important. If you choose a singular form, you should stick with it. The following appeared in the same paragraph about breakdown insurance:

✗ National Breakdown is recognised by over two and a half million members nationwide... National Breakdown are also the first nationwide motoring organisation...

Is it – or are they?

NOUNS INTO VERBS

There's a two-way traffic between nouns and verbs, when words which are considered as fixed in one or other pigeon-hole show a wilful disregard for their appointed place and float into the neighbouring one. Like most changes in language these shifts are out of the control of teachers, grammarians and dictionary compilers.

... the Princess Royal criticised those who "scapegoated particular families..."

(Independent on Sunday)

... someone who gets a real buzz from incentivising, counselling and coaching your staff to achieve.

(Kentucky Fried Chicken recruitment advertisement)

... [Rob Roy] outlaw and folk hero whose life story was messaged by Sir Walter Scott ...

(Guardian)

British Airways is trialling an in-flight interactive entertainment system ...

(Time Out)

Scapegoating, incentivising, messaging, trialling might all be objected to on the grounds that they sound awkward or ugly. But this is largely a question of familiarity. The last three are more recent than the first, and so may jar on the ear for that reason. Time heals, though. Going back less than fifty years we find a dispute raging over the use of the word 'contact' as a verb. Ernest Gowers in *The Complete Plain Words* wrote that 'The credentials of *to contact* are still in dispute between those who, like Sir Alan Herbert, think it a "loathsome" word, and those who hold, with Ivor Brown, that it can claim indulgence on the ground that "there is no word which covers approach by telephone, letter and speech, and *contact* is self-explanatory and concise".' Among other nouns-that-have-been-shamefully-forced-into-working-as-verbs Gowers cites *feature, glimpse, position, sense* and *signature* before adding that all these terms have 'long since found their way into the dictionaries' (as verbs).

And if time makes us wonder why a fuss was ever made about the use of certain nouns as verbs – a process which suggests that some current uses will eventually be just as acceptable (even *incentivise* ?) – then time also causes other usages to disappear altogether: who would now talk about 'signaturing' a document?

Other nouns that are currently (and sometimes contentiously) being used as verbs include: to access; to bin; to debut; to impact; to input; to parent; to premier(e); to rubbish.

⇨ (See under HYPHEN for compound nouns)

NUMBERS

Whether to write numbers as figures or as words is, in part, a matter of personal preference. There are, however, some conventions. Years (1066, 1996) are almost invariably presented in figure form, as are large sums of money (£50,000), large and precise numbers of people (population: 23,461), people's ages when in double figures, percentages (10 per cent), page numbers (p 3), and most measurements (325 feet).

High round numbers can obviously be presented more briefly by using a combination of figures and words or standard abbreviations (3 million; £1.5bn), but if exact numbers are required the writer will almost always use figures only:

On the old definition it [unemployment] fell by 16,700 to 3,234,000.

(The Independent)

There is more flexibility with low numbers. Some newspapers operate a cut-off system, putting numbers under ten as words but numbers from 11 upwards in figure form:

Edwards [Britain's world-record-breaking triple-jumper], in that case, missed clouds nine and ten and went straight to 11.

(The Times)

... husband Peter, 29, and daughters Jade, ten, and Holly, six...

(Sun)

Mixing words and figures sometimes produces an effect of inconsistency, as in he *Times* example above (where the writer could have put... straight to eleven). It is more acceptable to use a mixture when giving people's ages, using the ten-and-under / 11-and-over formula.

From a stylistic point of view it is better to write out a low number as a word if it occurs in the middle of a sentence:

Knight was fielding no more than three yards from West Indian star Benjamin ...

(Sun)

It is also better to avoid beginning a sentence with a number in figure form:

Nine out of 10 mortgage borrowers...

(Guardian)

Adjectives and nouns derived from numbers, such as *second, fifteenth*, should be shown as words rather than put in abbreviated form (*2nd, 15th*) except in informal usage or unless they form part of a date (15th September). High round numbers – *thousandth, millionth* – almost always appear in this form. Middling numbers can look cumbersome on the page whichever way they are presented:

She was the hundred and twenty third / 123rd visitor of the day to the stately home.

but the first (using words) is preferable for formal usage.

⇨ (See also DATES)

OBJECTIVE / SUBJECTIVE

Both adjectives are to do with point of view. An *objective* approach is one which is <u>unaffected by personal feelings</u>, <u>detached</u>:

From an objective angle he could see that the new by-pass being built near his house would benefit the whole town.

Subjective means <u>personal</u>, <u>taking one's feelings into account</u>:

But from a subjective viewpoint he resented the noise and pollution which the nearby road would cause.

OFFICIAL / OFFICIOUS

Official is a noun or adjective, and describes a <u>person or process which is properly authorised</u>:

We saw the Embassy official to obtain visas for the trip.

The adjective *officious*, by contrast, means <u>interfering</u>, with an overtone of fussiness.

"What are you two talking about?" he asked in his usual officious manner.

OLDER

⇨ See ELDER

ONE

One in the sense of an unspecified individual is found in formal and impersonal contexts:

One should not enter into such agreements without careful thought.

In most written and in almost all spoken contexts 'you' is the natural substitute:

If you're travelling abroad this summer be sure to check the local exchange rate before you go.

Despite its usefulness as impersonalising device in some languages (e.g. French) *one* should not be used an alternative to 'I' in English except in the most formal writing, and then only sparingly. In speech a string of 'ones' is likely to sound pompous:

One felt that one's efforts just hadn't been appreciated and that one was wasting one's time.

(American usage frequently begins a sentence with *one* and then shifts to 'him / his':

One could not foresee what his circumstances were going to be.

A disadvantage of this practice is that it may not be immediately clear whether the *one* and the 'him / his' are the same person.)

ONLY

Care needs to be taken over the placing of *only* in a sentence because the meaning of the sentence can change according to the position of the adverb:

1) Only I lent you the book yesterday.

(i.e. no one else lent it to you)

2) I only lent you the book yesterday.

(i.e. I didn't <u>give</u> it to you – although there is an ambiguity in the sentence and it could equally carry the sense of sentence [5])

3) I lent only you the book yesterday.

(i.e. I didn't want anyone else to have it)

4) I lent you the only book yesterday.

(i.e. the single copy I have)

5) I lent you the book only yesterday.

(i.e. and not two days before)

Not all of these sound equally natural or English (1 and 3 would probably be expressed in a different way). But the remainder provide an example of how changing the position of a single word, even slightly, changes meaning. There is usually no ambiguity in speech: the way something is said makes the meaning clear. And in written English the sense is generally clear enough, even if the word is misplaced. Nevertheless, getting *only* wrong contributes to the fuzziness of a piece of prose:

– **Paul Schrader, though only directing his first film...**

(Times)

(as opposed, say, to writing and photographing it as well. Better expressed as **directing only his first film**.)

There is only one proviso – we will only recruit the best.

(ad)

(We won't do anything else with them – only recruit them. Would have been slightly more accurate as **recruit only the best**)

ORAL

⇨ See AURAL

OVER-EXAGGERATE

Exaggerate means to <u>make extravagant or excessive claims</u>. Since the word contains the idea of going too far, to *over-exaggerate* is to overdo what is already overdone, and is an example of unnecessary repetition:

✗✗ **Officials from both parties claimed that the Tories were** over-exaggerating their poor prospects ...

(The Times)

⇨ (See REPETITION)

OVERTONE / UNDERTONE

These two nouns are, in practice, hardly to be distinguished. Both suggest something added, external to a piece of speech or writing, a book, a film, and so on, but giving extra meaning. As the word itself indicates, *overtone* has the suggestion of something relatively apparent, an outward effect achieved consciously or otherwise by its originator. An *undertone* may be harder to detect, because more pervasive and hidden rather than being consciously 'placed':

The manager's announcement of falling orders inevitably had grim overtones for his staff.

There is an undertone of melancholy in Charles Dickens's later novels.

OWING

⇨ See DUE TO

PARAGRAPH

HOW LONG?

The paragraph is a unit of sense in the same way that a phrase, or a clause, or a sentence is. Paragraphing isn't the arbitrary chopping up of a chunk of prose. There should be a reason why a particular paragraph runs to a hundred sentences – or is composed of only one sentence. This is another of those areas, however, where rules do not apply (or rather, do not even exist), and what follows is a series of observations.

1) Ending one paragraph and starting another suggests a change of direction, even if a slight one. A new subject, a fresh emphasis, the next stage in an argument or a narrative – all of these would probably require a new paragraph. And it's not just the content that should bother the writer. With paragraphing there is also an aesthetic consideration: how does the thing look on the page? A succession of lengthy paragraphs could put the reader off. A single block squatting on the page may look as unwelcoming as a tombstone on a hearthrug.

2) On the other hand (a classic and clichéd way of introducing a new paragraph), a cluster of short paragraphs perhaps hints at a certain nervousness on the writer's part. Like someone who talks fast for fear of losing the listener's attention, the writer who hops from one tiny paragraph to the next is frightened of stretching the reader's patience and good-will. Quick! Better get on to the next topic or he might turn the page. For this and other reasons, short paragraphs are much favoured by advertisers and the leader-writers and columnists in some newspapers. There is a real danger that we will turn the page here if points aren't made succinctly.

In fact, Franche-Comte is blessed with a range of culinary delights.

Bresi beef, smoked Luxeuil ham, Montbeliard sausage. Even the most parched mouth waters at the name.

And yet man cannot live by lunch alone. There are things to do and places to see.

(tourist advertisement)

Whisky makers are campaigning to have spirits advertised on the telly.

They seem to have a point, since beer makers do it all the time.

I like a drink. So for me to argue against alcohol is a bit like a stripper campaigning against nudity.

(Daily Star)

(Compressing these two examples into a single paragraph each – and this could very naturally have been done, since the sense of the sentences works together – would have strained the attention span of the reader. Or so the writers must have thought.)

3) Short paragraphs, each one or two sentences long, can work well when a limited amount of information has to be conveyed, a few important facts highlighted, or a simple opinion or argument advanced. But they may be counter-productive in a lengthy piece of writing. Just as the eye wants a bit of variety on the page, so the mind is more responsive to prose which uses different devices. Writing which is composed of nothing but one- or two-sentence paragraphs takes on a grasshopper quality.

4) As with sentences, paragraph length should be varied. Not in a mechanical way (short – long – short – long), but as a response to the overall structure of what is being said on the page. Here's a point that needs emphasising (and therefore a whole paragraph to itself); and here's a topic that is more complex (and so requires a couple of longer, more analytical paragraphs).

5) And, finally, here's something that can stand by itself – because it's the end of the piece, and what most readers want at the end is an economical but clinching statement.

DIALOGUE

It is the convention in dialogue writing to give a fresh paragraph to each new speaker:

'But,' Nately cried out in disbelief, 'you're a turncoat! A time-server!

A shameful, unscrupulous opportunist!'

'I am a hundred and seven years old,' the old man reminded him suavely.

'Don't you have any principles?'

'Of course not.'

'No morality?'

'Oh, I am a very moral man,' the villainous old man assured with satiric seriousness, stroking the hip of a buxom black-haired girl...

(Joseph Heller, Catch-22)

⇨ (See also QUOTATION MARKS)

PARENTHESES

⇨ See BRACKETS

PASSED / PAST

These two forms are sometimes confused. *Passed* is the past tense form of the verb *pass*:

The funeral cortege passed the gas-works.

Past is a noun:

The past is another country. *(L.P.Hartley)*

an adjective:

past times, past tense

an adverb:

the car sped past

and a preposition:

past its sell-by date

PATHETIC

⇨ See PITEOUS

PEACEABLE / PEACEFUL

There is a slight difference between the applications of these two adjectives. *Peaceable* means inclined to peace and describes an attitude, a person:

Both nations were essentially peaceable and a solution to the border dispute was found through negotiation.

Peaceful means quiet, not characterised by violence, and can describe places, pieces of music, etc., as well as individuals or nations:

We unplugged the phone and settled down for a peaceful evening.

PEDAL / PEDDLE

Pedal as a noun is a <u>lever worked by the foot</u>; as a verb it is to <u>operate such a</u> <u>lever</u>:

I pedalled fast to keep the other bikes in sight.

Pedaller is the associated noun (not very often seen).

Peddle, a verb, is to <u>sell small items</u>. When applied to any other kind of trade there is the suggestion of sleaziness or illegality: *peddling* lies, *peddling* drugs. A *pedlar* went from door to door selling goods; the practice may go on but the word has almost disappeared. The drug pusher or the supplier of doubtful information is a *peddler*.

PENINSULA / PENINSULAR

A *peninsula* is a <u>long area of land mostly</u> <u>surrounded by water but still</u> <u>connected to a bigger land mass</u>: **the Iberian Peninsula**. The adjectival form of the word adds '-r': **Peninsular Malaysia.**

PERCEPTIBLE / PERCEPTIVE / PERCIPIENT

The first two of these three adjectives are sometimes confused. *Perceptible* describes something which is probably quite slight but <u>can be seen</u>:

Surprisingly, the by-election result showed a perceptible shift in favour of the party in power.

Perceptive means <u>possessing insight</u>, <u>penetrating in judgement</u>:

Perceptive as usual, she uncovered the truth with a few deft questions.

Percipient, with the same sense of <u>penetrating</u> as *perceptive*, is less often found.

PEREMPTORY / PERFUNCTORY

Peremptory is an adjective meaning <u>abrupt</u>, <u>commanding</u>:

He barked a couple of peremptory orders and walked off.

Perfunctory, an adjective, means <u>hasty and superficial</u>:

With twenty documents to get through she gave only perfunctory treatment to each.

PERPETRATE / PERPETUATE

To *perpetrate* is <u>to carry out</u>, <u>to commit</u>.

The noun that follows the verb is almost always 'crime', 'outrage', etc.

The invasion of privacy was so outrageous it could have been perpetrated by the English, they said ...

(The Times)

To *perpetuate* is to sustain, to make last:

> **There is an abiding ideal of Japanese womanhood... perpetuated by the white-gloved elevator girls who bow to customers in department stores.**
>
> *(The Times)*

PERQUISITE / PREREQUISITE

A *perquisite* is a benefit arising from a job. The word is usually (and colloquially) shortened to *perk*, and would only be spelled out in full in fairly formal contexts:

> **Among the perquisites of this position are frequent foreign travel and a generous entertainment allowance.**

A *prerequisite* is a condition that must be met beforehand:

> **... cost-effective production and a strong balance sheet are merely the prerequisites for survival.**
>
> *(The Times)*

PERSECUTE / PROSECUTE

The two verbs are sometimes confused. To *persecute* is to maintain a campaign of harassment (particularly for political or religious reasons):

> **In Soviet Russia dissidents were persecuted and frequently imprisoned.**

To *prosecute* is to bring before a court of law:

> **First-time offenders may be warned by the police rather than prosecuted.**

(*Prosecute* has the less familiar meaning of to pursue in order to accomplish; in this sense a war or a political campaign can be *prosecuted*.)

PERVERSE / PERVERTED

Perverse describes a person or an action that is contrary, obstinate, something hard to account for rationally. It would be *perverse* to ask directions from someone in the street and then take a different turning to the one you had been told; *perverse* to eat one's meals in reverse, ending the day with breakfast.

The adjective is often used to describe a person's attitude to life:

> **Self-consciously perverse fellow that he was, he probably tore it** [a play manuscript] **up because his friend and champion liked it.**
>
> *(The Times)*

Perverted has a sexual application almost exclusively, and characterises behaviour or attitudes that are deviant. Even in such a notoriously vague area as sexual definition, *perverted* still carries some weight and is generally applied to activities that are not merely off the beaten track but are also offensive, and sometimes criminal. However, what is *perverted* to one man or woman may be another's standard liberated sexual behaviour. It is a staple term in some newspapers:

The perverted couple are proud of their executive client list.

(Sun)

The noun form *pervert* (with the stress on the first syllable) should be reserved for deserving cases, as it were, and not applied indiscriminately as a term of abuse.

As a verb *pervert* (stress on second syllable) is most frequently found in a legal context: to *pervert* the course of justice is to interfere with the proper process of the law (by threats, bribes, etc.).

PITEOUS / PITIABLE / PITIFUL / PATHETIC / (PATHOS)

The first three adjectives all mean arousing pity, although with very slight differences in usage. *Piteous* is not applied to individuals as such but to anything that moves us to feel pity:

The searchers heard the piteous sounds of the trapped cat.

Pitiable and *pitiful* can be applied to people and situations. Of the two *pitiful* is perhaps slightly stronger, suggesting someone who arouses pity through some visible means as well as by internal suffering, while *pitiable* is more to do with the latter:

There is moving testimony from the civilian survivors and the equally pitiable aircrew.

(The Times)

Both adjectives are also used to indicate mockery (a *pitiful* attempt).

Pathetic has a milder meaning of arousing sympathy, but usually carries an overtone, if not of contempt, then of superiority:

The opposing side made a pathetic sight after our victory.

The colloquial use of *pathetic* to mean useless, or, more casually, as a term passing judgement on an unsatisfactory situation, can sometimes be a source of ambiguity:

There are still oddities like the pathetic minority of women MPs...

(The Times)

(Here the writer isn't commenting on the quality of women MPs but on the unsatisfactory fact that there are so few of them.)

(The noun *pathos* denotes the quality that stirs up pity. The term is usually found in literary / artistic contexts, and indicates a conscious attempt on the part of an artist to move the audience, usually to tears. Charles Dickens, for example, was expert at manufacturing fictional scenes of *pathos* [frequently centring on the death of children], and the taste for such episodes emerges in different ways in different periods. Some of Walt Disney's cartoons contain scenes of *pathos*.)

PLUS

The use of plus to mean 'and':

We could get all the luggage plus the dog into the car.

is a colloquialism and should be avoided in formal writing. The noun use is slightly more acceptable, but other words like 'benefit', 'advantage', 'bonus', 'recommendation' can replace it:

A definite plus of the scheme is its low initial cost.

POLITIC / POLITICAL

The adjectives have distinct meanings although coming from the same root. *Politic* means calculating, shrewd, with an overtone of cunning:

In a politic move he sounded out individual committee members before putting the matter to a vote.

Political means to do with politics: *political* studies; *political* parties.

POLITICAL CORRECTNESS

The term 'politically correct', or PC, when applied to language describes the use of words or expressions whose purpose is to avoid giving offence. Political correctness is a display of sensitivity towards members of minority groups, and aims to eradicate the built-in tendency in language to stigmatise particular groups. A careful user of politically correct language would therefore avoid expressions such as 'mankind', 'turn a deaf ear', 'blind as a bat', 'seeing things in black and white', since they make casual reference to disability or colour or, in the case of 'mankind', appear to exclude half the world's population. (Humankind would be a more acceptable term.)

'Politically correct' is most often used as a term of abuse – that is, those who choose their words carefully so as to avoid giving offence or raising the spectres of sexism, racism, homophobia, etc., are attacked for their misplaced sensitivity, or their liberal 'softness', or their willingness to use expressions that sound ugly or absurd. Much fun is had with descriptions like 'horizontally challenged' (for large or fat) or 'differently abled' (for disabled). But the protesters themselves sometimes protest too much, and the very strong feelings roused by the subject indicate that there are more than words at issue here.

On the farther shores of political correctness absurdities do occur. In social work circles, for example, it is politically incorrect to ask to have your coffee black (say 'without milk', instead). You shouldn't say blackboard but chalkboard. This kind of tip-toeing around certain words gives the words themselves an extraordinary, almost magical, authority. It also fails to distinguish between something which is essentially neutral, as the 'black' in coffee is neutral, and an obviously pejorative application of the term ('black sheep', 'black as they're painted'). Avoiding one expression for good reasons doesn't mean one has to avoid them all, for no reason.

Similarly, it might seem straining things to insist that *history* become *herstory* or that *woman* loses her '-man' to become *womyn*. Or that *menstruation* change to *femstruation*, or *manhole* to *personhole* (or *femhole* or *personnel access structure*). On the wilder shores of PC it is, in fact, hard to distinguish between suggestions for changed terminology which are made in a spirit of sincerity, and those that are mischievously put forward to dicredit the whole business of Political Correctness. Nevertheless there are cases where certain expressions may be hurtful, insensitive and the like, and while it's not the job of a speaker or writer to avoid giving offence, it's not her (or his) job to alienate his (or her) audience either by the careless use of terms which a bit of thought might have found alternatives for.

POPULOUS / POPULAR

Populous indicates that an area is <u>densely populated</u> (all cities are *populous* by definition), while *popular* means <u>in favour</u>, <u>liked by many</u>.

(The noun *populace* means the <u>common people</u> and, for obvious reasons, tends to be applied in a historical context [the Roman populace] or to a population comfortably removed from the author by geography.)

PORE / POUR

The two verbs are sometimes confused. To *pore* is to <u>examine carefully</u>:

The couple also pored over a copy of the News of the World which had been pushed through their letterbox.

(Sun)

To *pour* is to <u>make flow</u>:

He was a generous host when it came to pouring drinks.

The usual mistake is to use this second word when the first is meant:

✗✗ As late as page 191 Augie is still pouring over magazines in search of "vocational hints".

(Guardian)

PRACTICE / PRACTISE

One of a group of word pairs which change by one letter between noun and verb. The *practice* with a 'c' is the noun:

... many parallels between Indian and British business practices.

(Independent)

while the *practise* with an 's' is the verb:

The band practised for most of the day.

(US usage is *practice* for both noun and verb.)

PRACTICAL / PRACTICABLE

A *practical* person or idea is a <u>sensible and realistic</u> one. When applied to a plan, it suggests that not only can it be realised but also that the plan has merits:

Within half an hour she came up with three practical ways of getting round the problem.

Practical carries the additional senses of <u>good at making things</u> and <u>down to earth</u> or <u>actual</u> (*practical* experience as opposed to theoretical knowledge).

Practicable is not used about people, and indicates merely that something <u>can be achieved</u>, and not necessarily that it ought to be. In this quotation it means that the slope is not too steep to climb down:

Below, down what was now a moonlit and practicable slope, he saw the dark and broken appearance of rock-strewn turf.

(H.G. Wells, The Country of the Blind)

(The adverb *practically* carries the additional sense of <u>almost, nearly</u>: as in **practically finished**. There is potential for a small ambiguity in a sentence such as **The map was practically useless** where the meaning could be either that the map was almost useless, or that it was useless for any practical purpose such as finding one's way – but could, for example, be hung on the wall as decoration.)

PRECEDE / PROCEED

Precede means <u>to go before</u>:

George I preceded George II.

Proceed is simply <u>to go forward</u>, <u>carry on</u>:

George III proceeded to go mad.

PRECEDING / PROCEEDING

Preceding is used as an adjective to mean <u>going before</u>:

The committee took up the unfinished business of the preceding day.

Proceeding must never be used in this context. It is the present participle of *proceed* or a noun (usually in the plural) meaning an <u>action</u> or <u>event</u>:

The next morning, memories of the night's proceedings filled her with dismay.

PRECEDENCE / PRECEDENT

Precedence means <u>priority</u>:

The oldest members of the club took precedence when it came to the best chairs.

A *precedent* is a <u>past instance</u>. Its most usual application is in the law, where an earlier judgement works as a guide to similar situations that arise later, but *precedent* can be applied to anything in the past which serves as an example for the present, or to something occurring now which sets a pattern for the future:

> **A precedent was set in the Long Room at Lord's on Thursday evening when Julian Bream** [the classical guitarist]... gave a **recital.**
>
> *(The Times)*

(*Precedent* is more often found in a negative context: 'without *precedent* ', or in the adjectival '*unprecedented*'.)

PRECIPITATE / PRECIPITOUS

Precipitate, as an adjective, describes an action that is <u>rushed,</u> <u>headlong</u>:

> **... in the face of this onslaught the British units were in precipitate retreat ...**
>
> *(The Times)*

As a verb it means <u>to produce abruptly</u>:

> **... the idea that psychological stress can precipitate sudden death ...**
>
> *(The Times)*

Precipitous means <u>steep</u>:

> **The [railway] cutting was extremely deep, and unusually precipitous ...**
>
> *(Dickens, The Signalman)*

However, *precipitous* is quite frequently used to describe an action which, in strict correctness, should be called *precipitate*:

> ✗ **... the precipitous rush by stores to forsake the high street in return for out-of-town sites ...**
>
> *(The Times)*

There is still some life, and value, in the difference between *precipitate* and *precipitous*, and the distinction is worth preserving.

PREREQUISITE / PERQUISITE

⇨ See PERQUISITE / PREREQUISITE

PREPOSITION

Prepositions are small linking words that are put in front of, usually, nouns or pronouns, and indicate the relationship between that noun and another word. Prepositions include such words as 'under', 'on', 'after', 'by', 'to', 'from', 'through'.

THE RIGHT PREPOSITION

Care should be taken to use the appropriate preposition in a particular context.
In part, this is a matter of convention:

✗ [she] **won't lay that pistol down until she's avenged herself of the man
who murdered her father.**

   (Guardian)

(You avenge yourself *on* somebody *for* something that has been done against
you. The use of *of* after 'avenge' is marked as 'archaic' in the Oxford English
Dictionary.)

I was really bored of it by that time.

('bored of' is a very popular expression, but the conventional phrase is 'bored
with'.)

PREPOSITION AT THE END OF A SENTENCE

The old convention that one shouldn't end a sentence with a preposition has
been a long time dying. Like the 'rule' that no infinitive should ever be split it
is an example of false correctness, and had its origins in the fact that Latin does
not end its sentences with prepositions. There is a well-known anecdote about
what Winston Churchill wrote on the margin of a report in which an official
had studiously avoided prepositions at the ends of sentences: 'This is the sort
of bloody nonsense up with which I will not put'.

The best guide over the placing of the preposition is what sounds natural.
One shouldn't be doctrinaire and insist that all prepositions – or none – come
at the end. For example, in the last sentence but two, putting the preposition at
the end would have produced an ugly and confusing piece of English: '...the
margin of a report which an official had studiously avoided prepositions at the
ends of sentences in'. In many cases, however, it is appropriate, in spoken and
written English, to put the preposition at the end of the sentence:

Now is the time to see this, and your head is the place to see it in.

   (Martin Amis)

They are dorks and geeks whom she wouldn't be seen dead with.

   (Daily Telegraph)

**We have to challenge teachers to abandon the "progressive" ideas
some still cling to.**

   (The Times)

Changing the words around in these examples so that the preposition came in
the middle would not produce 'better' sentences but, arguably, ones that were
slightly stilted. The sentence which could be most easily changed is the last
and most 'formal' (**...the "progressive" ideas to which some still cling**).

If formality is important it may be worth recasting the sentence so that the
preposition is not left hanging on or over at the end. Even in less formal

writing a sentence should be reshaped if there is a long gap between the word to which the preposition applies and the preposition itself:

Crickhowell House... which, it is claimed, a quango has been forced to pay above market rent for.

(photo caption, Independent on Sunday)

(13 words come between the relative *which* and the preposition *for*. A tighter construction would be... for which, it is claimed,...)

Awareness of the preposition 'rule' and the wish to sound formal and correct sometimes sit uneasily with natural usage, particularly in speech, and people get tangled up and repeat the preposition:

'When you're buying a basic utility about which none of us can do anything about at the moment...'

(interviewee on Radio 4)

(This kind of sentence is a classic instance of where the natural word order – **This isn't a situation which we can do anything about** – is preferasble to the stilted: **This isn't a situation about which we can do anything.**)

PRESCRIBE / PROSCRIBE

To *prescribe* is to <u>direct</u>, to <u>lay down as a rule</u>:

The doctor prescribed plenty of rest and exercise.

To *proscribe* is to <u>ban</u>:

The government is attempting to proscribe hard-core pornography channels on satellite television.

(The nouns forms are, respectively, *prescription* and *proscription*. This second word is fairly rare.)

PRESUMPTUOUS / PRESUMPTIVE

Presumptuous means <u>arrogant</u>, <u>impudent</u>:

He was presumptuous enough to think he could answer for the whole group without consulting anybody.

Presumptive means <u>giving grounds for presuming,</u> <u>likely</u>:

We've made some forecasts on the basis of this year's presumptive profits.

(The heir *presumptive* is the individual who will succeed to a title, etc. unless anybody more closely related to the present possessor is born. The phrase is also used to describe the person who is generally considered most likely to obtain some prominent position.)

⇨ (See also ASSUME / PRESUME)

PRINCIPAL / PRINCIPLE

Principal is both noun and adjective, and means <u>chief</u>, <u>most important</u>:

The principal things to remember, he was told, were to keep his speech short and relevant.

The most usual application of the noun is to describe the <u>head of a college or a school</u> (this is particularly a US usage), or to refer to the <u>main actor(s)</u> in a play or singers in a musical production. An additional noun meaning of *principal* is <u>money on which interest is paid</u>.

Principle is a noun only, and means <u>basic truth</u>:

There are principles here, they insist, and they should be examined before too much is give away.

(Guardian)

The word can also be used in the sense of <u>guiding idea</u>:

Business Class is a new arrival in Russia, although the principle of better treatment for the few is not.

(The Times)

PROCEED

⇨ See PRECEDE

PROCEEDING

⇨ See PRECEDING

PROGRAM / ME

In America all *programs*, theatre, TV, computer, are just that – *programs*. British English differentiates between the *programme* in the theatre, on TV etc., and the *program* on the computer.

PRONE / SUPINE

As descriptions of bodily positions *prone* means <u>face-down</u>, on one's front, while *supine* is <u>lying on one's back</u>, face-up. They carry additional meanings of, respectively, <u>tending towards</u> (**prone to depression**) and <u>passive</u> (**He's so supine – he never raises any objections.**)

PRONOUNS

Pronouns raise problems of formal and informal use. There are differences between the two styles of using English pronouns, mostly those involving I / me, but some people over-compensate when speaking or writing in a 'correct' way, and in the attempt to be right in fact make mistakes.

WHEN I GO SECOND

It is the convention to put the first person pronoun ('I') second or last in any list. It's a form of word-order politeness – after you; no, after you. In speech and in colloquial writing it is quite usual to find the order reversed, and the first person pronoun placed in front. Where this happens the *I* is almost invariably turned into *me*:

Me and Madonna, you know, we're just so misunderstood.

(The Times)

This is not acceptable in formal writing (or indeed in any kind of formal speaking), where *I* should always be at the end of the queue:

you and I; he, she and I.

This applies only where the pronouns form the subject of the sentence. When they are the object then *I* must turn into *me*:

The dog turned his forlorn eyes on her and me.

Some root-memory of the correctness of the word-order *you and I* often causes the phrase to be transferred unchanged (and wrongly) when it is the object of a verb or when it comes after a preposition. The principal offending phrase is *between you and I* which is always incorrect. It can only be *between you and me*. The same mistake is found with other prepositions:

✗✗... **"a richer retailing environment" – better shops to you and I.**

(The Times)

✗✗More and more families may be splitting apart but unless it happens to you or I...

(Time Out)

(**you and me** in both cases. It is helpful to see if the phrase still works after removing the *you and...* element; e.g. *better shops to... I* or *happens to... I*. It then becomes obvious if *I* is wrong.)

I OR ME?

The gap between formal and informal usage of the personal pronouns, such as *I / me, she / her*, is shown most obviously in the simplest sentence: **It's me**. This is technically wrong, as *me* is neither the object of a verb nor follows a preposition (as it does, for example, in: **They saw me** or **He spoke to me**).

The correct rendering of **It's me** would therefore be **It is I**, but it would be a pedantic speaker who went round announcing himself like this all the time. However, in English which is written with any degree of formality one should put: **It was I who first drew your attention to...**

Similarly, spoken phrasing like **We thought it was her who had the idea** should change, in written English, to... it was she who had...

Expressions like **me and my friend** are acceptable only in informal speech and writing:

> **...a Romeo and Juliet for the Nineties was played out as a couple sauntered by, him in black and white, her in the red of Manchester United ...**
>
> *(Independent)*

The relaxed, colloquial tone the writer adopts here is signalled by the use of *him* and *her* where *he* and *she* would be grammatically right.

But before using pronouns in this (incorrect) way the writer needs to be certain of his or her intended audience, as well as ensuring that the style is suitable to the subject matter. The grammatically correct form will be appropriate most of the time.

MYSELF

Myself is used for emphasis:

> **I myself would not choose that option.**

It is unnecessary to put *myself* in place of *I* or *me* in sentences like:

✗ Neither my brother nor myself have seen him for months.

> *(... neither my brother nor I...)*

✗ He said he would get in touch with my brother or myself.

> *(... with my brother or me...)*

PRONOUN STRINGS

Too many pronouns can cause uncertainty about who, exactly, is intended to be who:

✗ Bill said he'd spoken to Pete and he'd told him he really shouldn't do anything about it until he considered the odds were in his favour.

> *(Which 'he' is which?)*

✗ Bed Dust Mites hate Sleep Rite Pillows – because they have difficulty in penetrating them they are healthier to use.

> *(an advertisement in which 'they' applies to both mites and pillows)*

⇨ (See also WHO / WHOM)

PROPHECY / PROPHESY

Prophecy, meaning <u>prediction</u> and pronounced to rhyme with 'see', is a noun:

> **The sect's prophecy that the world was about to end was generally ignored.**

To *prophesy*, to <u>foretell</u>, is a verb (pronounced to rhyme with 'sigh'). The verb doesn't carry quite the religious / messianic overtones of the noun, and can be used in the sense of forecast:

The company prophesied continued growth for the rest of the year.

(The c / s difference between noun and verb also applies to ADVICE / ADVISE, DEVICE / DEVISE, LICENCE / LICENSE, PRACTICE / PRACTISE)

PUNCTUATION IN DIRECT SPEECH

Punctuation within quoted sentences is absolutely normal; problems arise only where the break comes between direct speech and the rest of the narrative.

In direct speech punctuation which is related to the words actually said (commas, full stops, exclamation marks, etc.) is included <u>within</u> the quotation marks:

"I don't see why. I didn't know I was doing anything wrong."

"You committed bigamy. That's a terrible crime."

(all examples from Anthony Burgess, <u>Devil of a State</u>)

When the speaker is identified and a verb such as 'said', 'shouted', 'whispered' is tagged onto the piece of direct speech, a comma separates the speech from the rest of the sentence:

"You've got to take your medicine," said Mudd very grimly.

The comma is placed <u>inside</u> the quotation marks. If the sentence structure were switched around so that the speaker's name and the speech-word came first – **Mudd said very grimly, "You've got to take your medicine."** – the comma would be placed before the quotation marks.

Question marks and exclamation marks are followed by lower-case letters, not capitals, if the words that come after are part of the same sentence:

"But is she still alive?" asked Mudd.

"Boy!" called Rowlandson.

A capital letter begins each fresh sentence within a single block of speech even if the speaker remains the same:

"Cheer up," said Lydgate. "You've got a lot to celebrate."

(Two sentences here, one beginning **Cheer up...**, the other **You've got...**)

But when the identity of the speaker and the speech word ('said', 'shouted') interrupt a single sentence of dialogue, then commas are used on both sides of the interruption and a lower-case letter begins the second chunk of dialogue:

"Oh, Frank, Frank," said Lydia, a small handkerchief at her weeping nose, "how could you? What do I do now?"

The exception to the rules and conventions outlined above comes when you are incorporating into a piece of writing a brief quotation (not a complete sentence) whose conclusion coincides with the end of your own sentence. Here the final full-stop can be placed <u>outside</u> the quotation marks:

They deceive their husbands and discover, in the words of Thomas Hardy, that true love can only grow in "the interstices of a harsh,

prosaic reality".

(The Times)

If a speech extends beyond a single paragraph, for example when a single speaker is telling a story, the convention is to leave out the quotation marks at the end of each paragraph but to include them at the beginning of the next paragraph to show that one speaker is at work, as here:

"... and not a soul wants someone else's child to suffer the same thing.

"It's really like nothing I've ever seen in my twenty-two years of police work..."

(Patricia Cornwell, The Body Farm)

QUESTION MARK

A question mark must be used in direct speech:

'Is there anybody there?' said the Traveller,
Knocking on the moonlit door

(Walter de la Mare)

Note, however, that the question mark is <u>not</u> used in indirect speech. Turned into indirect speech, and made flat and unpoetic, these lines would read:

Knocking on the moonlit door, the traveller asked if anybody was there *(without a question mark)*

⇨ (See also PUNCTUATION IN DIRECT SPEECH and REPORTED SPEECH)

A question mark is used in ordinary prose, even if the question itself is not spoken aloud:

Where does he stand in the game?

(The Times)

When was the last time you snuggled up with a thrusting indictment of the Danish educational system circa 1971?

(Independent on Sunday)

Rhetorical questions – that is, questions which aren't really questions but statements with which the writer / speaker expects his or her audience to agree – also require a question mark:

What could be more tedious than to hear that someone has been sacked or stuck on the M25?

(Independent)

Why the heck are we feather-bedding vermin like him?

(Sun)

Statements which are cast in the form of questions as part of the tactics of conversation – **'Nice day today, isn't it.', 'But I'm not going to do it, am I.'** – can drop the question mark. When spoken aloud neither of these statements would be delivered with the voice rising at the end of the sentence or a voice that would suggest uncertainty, one of the marks of a true question. The best guide as to whether a question mark is necessary in writing is to 'voice' the remark inside one's head. That generally makes clear the difference between a question and, say, an exclamation, even if the words used are the same in either case:

There aren't enough of them to go round, are there?

There aren't enough of them to go round, are there!

Questions marks are also used to indicate uncertainty over factual information:

Bormann, Martin (1900 – 1945?)

This entry in a biographical dictionary indicates doubt over whether the Nazi leader Bormann really died in 1945. (This was the last date on which he was 'officially' alive but there were repeated sightings in South America.)

And, used in conjunction with brackets, the question mark conveys the author's doubt or raises a possibility:

This gives Caruso... ample opportunity for exercising his (only?) trademark facial expression ...

(Independent on Sunday)

QUOTATION MARKS

1) Quotation marks are generally used to indicate direct speech:

'Everyone thinks Edward is at Quitterne,' said Harry. That was the name of the McCaskervilles' country cottage. 'But you say he isn't.'

'He isn't!'

'All right, I believe you!'

'Then why do you say "I say" he isn't?'

(Iris Murdoch, The Philosopher's Pupil)

Single quotation marks are the convention in novels, although speech reproduced elsewhere, in newspapers for example, may use double marks. However, quotation within a piece of dialogue (as **"I say"** in the last line above) is frequently signified by double marks. If double quotation marks are already being used for the principal piece of speech, then whatever is quoted within the speech should be enclosed within <u>single</u> marks, so as to distinguish it from the rest of the sentence:

Ken joked: "I told my sons after I'd won that on my gravestone they'll have to put, 'He did it in the end'."

(Daily Star)

⇨ (See also DIALOGUE)

2) Quotation marks can be used to stress that the words reproduced appear exactly as they were said:

Mr Blackwood, who misses Britain "like you would miss toothache",
then moved into private waste disposal.

(The Times)

3) Single quotation marks are used for titles of short poems and stories and
songs:

Robert Frost's 'The Road Not Taken';

The Beatles' 'I Wanna Hold Your Hand'.

The other uses of quotation marks involve the putting of some distance
between an author and his or her words. It's as if the words inside the
quotation marks were being handled with tongs.

4) They may cast doubt on the descriptive correctness of a statement:

**But although he scrambled on top of the kitchen sink to improve his
view, the "saucer" had vanished behind cloud seconds before.**

(The Times)

(i.e. the writer doubts that there really was a flying saucer out there)

What the 'Conservative' press says

(Independent on Sunday headline)

(i.e. look at what the supposedly Conservative press is saying against the
Conservative Party)

**And what was I supposed to say when my son laughed out loud at
"jokes" about the sexual practices of female relatives of the
Southampton players?**

(Independent)

(the writer does not share her son's sense of humour)

5) Quotation marks are also used to suggest that the writer is dealing with
language or concepts he is unused to. Slang is sometimes treated in this way,
occasionally with an ironic slant, but more often to signal the specialist use of a
word:

**Mad Frank...is back in his old "manor" selling tickets to hear his life
story.**

(Independent)

(Here the quotation marks are necessary to show that *manor* is being used in its
police / underworld sense of 'district'.)

Some writers put quotation marks round a piece of slang or a colloquial usage
that makes them feel faintly uncomfortable:

He went on to 'nick' five more televisions.

It's just a "stone's throw" away from London.

(advertisement)

This suggests that the writer is aware of the colloquialism but is unable or unwilling to find another way of expressing himself. Anybody who is going to use slang or colloquial language, and considers that the use is appropriate for his audience, subject matter, etc., should be unapologetic about it – using quotation marks simply draws attention to the writer's unease. It's a verbal blush.

6) Jargon or specialised technical language may be cordoned off with quotation marks, a use that is related to 5) but also distinct because the terms don't fall into the category of slang:

> **If any Iraqi radar screen, for some unknown reason not already 'totalled' by the Allied air forces, chose to 'illuminate', it was to be immediately attacked.**
>
> *(Frederick Forsyth, The Fist of God)*

7) Made-up words are usually put between quotation marks:

> **He** [Winston Churchill] **said later that he had 'ratted' on the Tories, and when he returned to the Tory fold, he said he had 're-ratted'.**
>
> *(Observer)*

(Here the first set of marks round 'ratted' indicates a slang term, which you would find in many dictionaries, while the marks round 're-ratted' signify a variant expression made up for the occasion, a term that wouldn't appear in any dictionary.)

8) Quotation marks, single or double, are used between a first and a last name to indicate the nick-name a person may be known by:

> **Sir Henry 'Chips' Channon once moaned in his diaries ...**
>
> *(The Times);*
>
> **Elle "The Body" Macpherson**

9) There is a use of quotation marks which is half mocking, half ironic, and almost impossible to describe because it has to do with tone of voice and with attitude. This use hints at a joke shared between speaker and audience:

> **'In the new world of Quentin Tarantino and others, where everything is a pastiche and nothing is real, there are no more existential heroes, only "existential heroes" in inverted commas, who "love" the girl, or "kill" the girl, but are winking at you the whole time.'**
>
> *(film director Paul Schrader, quoted in the Independent)*

REASON IS... BECAUSE

An example of tautology. *Reason* does not need to be followed by *because*, since the word already indicates that an explanation is going to be given. Although the *reason...because* coupling is usual in spoken English it should be avoided in formal use:

The reason he was late was because the train broke down.

(Substitute **that** for **because** or, more simply, put: **He was late because the train broke down.**)

It is also unnecessary to write **The reason why he was late...** – *why*, like *because*, promises an explanation which has already been signalled by the use of *reason*.

REBUT / REFUTE

The two verbs, meaning to <u>disprove by argument</u>, are almost interchangeable:

'I put a position, rebut it, refute the rebuttal, and rebut the refutation.'
(Tom Stoppard, quoted in the Guardian)

If there is a shade of difference between the two it is that *rebut* is the more aggressive, since the word still carries something of its old sense of <u>to ward off an attack</u>. *Rebut* and *refute* aren't the same as *deny*, which means merely <u>to say that something isn't so</u> (without the attempt at proof or disproof).

RECOURSE / RESOURCE / RESORT

The three words are closely linked, and a dictionary will usually define them in terms of each other. However, there are small differences in their usage. To have *recourse* to something means to go to it as a <u>source of aid</u>:

We had recourse to the Russian speaker in our group when we landed at the airport.

Resort can be used as verb in the sentence above (**We resorted to...**), giving the same meaning. This is more usual than the equivalent noun construction (**We had resort to...**).

A *resource* is also a <u>source of help</u>, but the word doesn't usually convey the idea that one has turned to something in an emergency or a difficulty; more often it carries the related sense of a <u>means</u> that one can draw on (a means of financial support, of filling one's time):

Time didn't hang on his hands after retirement: he had plenty of resources.

Resource is also a verb, often in participle form: **a properly resourced library**.

REGRETFUL / REGRETTABLE

The two adjectives are fairly easily confused. *Regretful* relates only to people who are <u>capable of showing regret</u>:

Under cross-examination the defendant claimed to be regretful over

what he had done.

Regrettable applies to incidents or situations (but not people) which are causing regret:

Then, in a regrettable turn of events, the company decided to close the factory.

The same distinction applies to the adverbs:

Regretfully, she closed the front door for the last time.

The announcer said that, regrettably, no more trains would run that day.

RELIGIOUS / RELIGIOSE

Religious has a straightforward application: connected to religion, godly.
Religiose is an adjective with a critical sense: sentimentally religious.

REPETITION

Repetition – using the same words or phrases within a short space of time – can be a useful stylistic effect, or it can be the result of not attending closely enough to what one is saying. Public speakers, particularly politicians, use repetition as one of the weapons in their armoury of effects. President Kennedy at his Inauguration Address (in January 1960) talked of the future:

'So let us begin anew – Let us never negotiate out of fear. But let us never fear to negotiate.

– 'All this will not be finished in the first hundred days. Nor will it be finished in the first one thousand days, nor in the life of this Administration, nor even perhaps in our lifetime on this planet. But let us begin.'

Repetition can be used to inspire. It can also undermine. In *Julius Caesar* by Shakespeare, Mark Antony, speaking to the Roman mob after Caesar's assassination, wishes to cast doubt on the motives on the men who killed Caesar. By repeatedly labelling them as 'honourable' (ten times in an interrupted speech), he suggests that they are in fact driven by dishonourable motives like envy or hatred. Any word or phrase used again and again draws the audience's attention and starts to look odd. So President Kennedy, in the passage quoted above, uses the formula **Let us + (verb)** just often enough to set up a rhythm in what he says, but not often enough to distract the audience from the vaguely uplifting content.

Repetition in skilful hands is a calculated effect, especially where it is combined with variation in sentence length:

Selina and I are very well suited. We get along like nobody's business. I must marry Selina. If I don't, I'll just die. If I don't, no one else will, and I'll have ruined another life. If I don't, I think she might sue me

for every penny I have.

(Martin Amis, Money)

But repetition can also make for monotonous reading or listening. A string of sentences which begin in the same way or the over-use of a single expression helps to produce uninteresting prose.

⇨ (See TAUTOLOGY)

REPORTED SPEECH

Reported or indirect speech is a way of conveying what has been said without the use of speech marks. A sentence employing direct speech such as the following:

He asked me, "Are you coming over here this afternoon?"

becomes in reported speech:

He asked me whether I was going over there that afternoon.

The quotation marks vanish. So does the question mark. Pronouns change (the **you** becomes **I** in the reported version). **Here** turns into **there; this afternoon** becomes **that afternoon. Coming** turns into **going**, because the point of view of the person producing the reported speech is taken into account. Most important, the tenses alter. The present in direct speech becomes the past in reported speech (**"I am watching TV." / She said she was watching TV**) while the future becomes the conditional 'would' (**"I will turn it off" / She said she would turn it off.**)

Some writers use reported speech to vary their prose. Miles Kington, in the following extract, had given several lines of direct speech before slipping into this reported passage:

... so I asked a friend called Mary if I could come and see myself on her set, and she said, fine, but she would be out that evening and her mother would be in. Fine, I said, as long as she doesn't mind watching as well. Not at all, said Mary, as long as you realise that my mother consumes a lot of sherry and will be well away by then, but just ignore her.

(Independent)

In fact, Kington moves back into direct speech for the last two sentences. He just happens not to use speech marks because they would break up the way the paragraph works as a single unit.

RESORT / RESOURCE

⇨ See RECOURSE

RESPECTABLE / RESPECTFUL / RESPECTIVE

Respectable has a range of meanings including worthy of respect (a *respectable* innings), <u>decent</u> (a *respectable* neighbourhood) and <u>good enough</u> (a *respectable* income).

Respectful means <u>showing respect for</u>:

The new office block was neither interesting nor respectful of the architectural heritage of the rest of the street.

Respective (more usually found in its adverbial form *respectively*) is used where items in two lists are being matched up, and indicates that the first thing in list a) is paired with first thing in list b), and so on:

The Specialist, starring Sylvester Stallone and Sharon Stone, as, respectively, an explosives expert and a revenge-seeker ...

(Guardian)

(Although *respectively* is often used unecessarily, in the example above it does help to clarify the sentence. Without it, the meaning could be that Sharon Stone plays both the explosives expert and the revenge-seeker. Well, it's possible...)

RESTFUL / RESTIVE / RESTLESS

Restful means <u>soothing</u>, <u>tranquil</u>, and is applied, not to people, but to experiences or objects that may have a calming effect, such as holidays or music:

Debussy's L'Apres-midi d'un Faune is a restful piece of music.

Restive describes someone <u>twitchy</u>, <u>reluctant to be controlled</u>:

The Prime Minister challenged the more restive Tory MPs to accept that Britain had a strategic interest ...

(Independent)

There is more than a shade of difference between the adjectives *restive* and *restless*. This latter word means simply <u>unable to stay</u> <u>still</u>; unlike *restive* it does not imply that anyone is attempting to exercise control:

Algy is certainly restless... He must dash off on impulse ...

(The Times)

RIGHT

The use of 'right' as a pretty well meaningless interjection is common in speech:

"So I get up, right, have a shower, right, then I'm out the door."

but should be avoided in any relatively formal speech or writing.

⇨ (See also LIKE)

SARCASM

⇨ See IRONY

SEASONAL / SEASONABLE

Both adjectives derive from *season* but have distinct applications. *Seasonal* means of / depending on the season:

All the hotels experience seasonal variations in their takings.

Seasonable means appropriate to the season:

Donning a seasonable white beard, he presented the children with their Christmas presents.

SEMI-COLON

The semi-colon provides a break between the different parts of sentence, and is used when a writer requires a stronger pause than a comma but wishes to avoid breaking up what is being said into separate and distinct sentences.

Extensively used in eighteenth and nineteenth century writing, the semi-colon has waned in popularity since then, perhaps because it is regarded as a fiddly piece of punctuation or simply a redundant one. It would be possible to pass a whole life without comitting a semi-colon to paper. A pity, because this piece of punctuation, in good hands, works as an elegant bridge between statements which could stand separately but which the writer has chosen to weave together:

It did not need the mouse nor her condition to bring Diana to his mind; she was there a great deal of the time; but it did tend to bring these wandering thoughts – recollections of her in former days, riding over the English countryside with singular grace and spirit; images of her in India, at the Institut, in the streets of Paris – to a sharper focus.

(Patrick O'Brian, The Surgeon's Mate)

Repeated use of the semi-colon can produce sentences which are over-extended. Again, a good writer will vary sentence length; after the passage quoted above, Patrick O'Brian uses a sentence of only seven words, then one of thirteen words.

The semi-colon sometimes gives a clipped appearance to prose, as if the writer were providing for us the minimum information required:

The menu was Pacific Rim; the noise deafening; the clientele movie-industry hopeful.

(Michael Crichton, Rising Sun)

DIFFERENCE BETWEEN COLON AND SEMI-COLON

It is not always easy to judge whether a semi-colon or a colon is more appropriate. In general, a semi-colon will take the place of a conjunction (and / but / because, etc.):

Alan Bond must regret the day he won the America's Cup for his country; it was the start of a long and painful decline.

(The Times)

(**because** / **as** / **since** could have been substituted for the semi-colon here, just as **for** / **and** could have been used in the examples from the two novels given above)

A semi-colon doesn't promise the explanation or amplification that comes with the colon, and the sentence it interrupts is sequential rather than having 'balanced' halves. For these reasons a colon would have been preferable in the following:

✗ There are metal casks, yet we still make the wooden ones; hogsheads, kilderkins, firkins, and the like.

    (Brewery advert)

(the second part of the sentence lists the wooden casks the firm still makes)

✗ The town occupies the Truckee Meadows, a spacious valley enclosed by sunny, snow-capped slopes; the Sierra Nevada rises in the west and the Virginia Range in the east.

    (The Times)

(the second part 'explains' what the snow-capped ranges are)

On the other hand, a colon might be preferable here:

Barry White does not just have a headache; he has a migraine.

    (The Times)

(the even-handed quality of this sentence would be enhanced by a colon – perhaps. This is one of those cases where selection of punctuation is a matter of choice rather than of correctness.)

Here, two sentences provide the contrast. In the first a semi-colon reinforces the objection signalled by the conjunction 'but', while in the second the colon marks an opening-out of the first part of the sentence:

Old wrongs don't cancel out new ones; but we do seem to be suffering from demob sulkiness. We need another struggle: new pinnacles to set our eyes on.

    (Libby Purves, The Times)

SENSUAL / SENSUOUS

Sensual is most often used to mean <u>sexual</u> (or simply <u>sexy</u>), and is in effect a euphemism for the more direct adjective. It sometimes carries a vague note of condemnation and, like 'erotic', it draws a teasing, semi-respectable veil over sex, and is often used as a come-on word in headlines and so on:

Sensual couples' joy of sinks hits dishwasher makers

    (Guardian headline over article which stated that French couples find that washing up together strengthens relationship).

Sensuous, although sometimes used as a synonym for *sensual*, has a wider meaning: <u>appealing to several of the senses</u>. A concert, a visit to an art gallery may be a *sensuous* experience – just as a good meal would be.

SENTENCE

WHAT IS IT?

The *sentence* is remarkably hard to define. Various descriptions of it can be made (some are given below) but grasping exactly what the *sentence* is can be an almost intuitive process.

Attempts at defining the *sentence*:

A *sentence* contains a finite verb. *(See under **Verb** in Glossary, page187)*

A *sentence* is a set of words 'making a complete grammatical structure, generally begun with a capital letter and ended with a full stop or its equivalent' (Chambers Dictionary).

A *sentence* is the expression of a single thought.

A *sentence* is any group of words concluded by a full stop.

Each of these statements, including this one, is a *sentence*.

If the *sentence* is as hard to describe as an elephant to someone who had never seen that animal before, it is nevertheless fairly easy to recognise – again, like the elephant. A working definition would be that a *sentence* is a group of words which, standing alone, make sense.

She should donate her lips to medical science.

(Sun)

makes sense, and is a *sentence* of a pretty simple cat-sat-on-the-mat variety, with a subject, verb, object (and indirect object).

A slightly more complicated sentence is:

There is a massive black hole at the centre of our galaxy, according to calculations by scientists in America

(The Times).

Here the first dozen words, up to the comma, contain the principal information and could stand by themselves as a *sentence*:

There is a massive black hole at the centre of our galaxy.

The second part:

according to calculations by scientists in America

does not make sense without the preceding information and is not a *sentence* – it has no verb, for one thing.

HOW LONG?

There are no rules about how long a sentence <u>ought</u> to be. A sentence that stretches a reader's patience or powers of understanding is too long – but sometimes ten words are enough to do both of these things.

The sports writer of the following just about keeps control:

An Everton side yesterday deprived for most of the second half of their £4m signing from Rangers, Duncan Ferguson – who was sent off after

> 54 minutes for an aggressive push on John Jensen – still managed to
> expose the flaws of an Arsenal team supposedly strengthened by the
> appearance of John Hartson, bought for £2.5m from Luton, and Chris
> Kiwomya, signed from Ipswich for a fee still to be agreed and used
> only briefly yesterday as a substitute.
>
> *(Independent on Sunday)*

Some writers take positive pleasure in long sentences, putting them through
their paces, cracking the whip. But the ending may be so delayed that the
reader has to go back to the beginning to check what the whole thing was
meant to be about:

> Both of these scraps were to be found in Paris, and were taken from
> the *Herald Tribune* (oh, yes, I munch my fodder where I find it, though
> I do acknowledge, and anyway years ago I used to write regularly for
> the *Trib* so they would forgive me, to say nothing of the fact that the
> *Trib* would probably be pleased by the sideways compliment), and I
> must give you an idea of what these two stories hold for us.
>
> *(Bernard Levin, The Times)*

Short sentences are favoured by advertisers and leader writers in newspapers.
They are punchy. They are good for making simple points simply. Sometimes
they aren't proper sentences at all. Just phrases. Like this.

> They've got a brilliant new law in California. Commit three violent
> offences and you get 25 years in jail. We should try it here.
>
> *(Sun)*

> And it isn't the only car to come with ABS. Full-size driver's airbag.
> Alloy wheels. Electric sunroof. And an immobiliser and alarm.
>
> *(advertisement)*

Broadcast language also favours brief sentences ("Today is a crunch day for
the government.") and non-sentences ("And now the weather.").

Repeated short sentences can deteriorate into an irritating mannerism as a
writer strives to convey just how serious and tense is his subject matter. It is
macho writing, pushed through clenched teeth:

> Something disturbs me. Wakes me. Pitch black. I listen. Outside.
> Banging. I get up. Move towards the window. It stops. Silence. I go
> back to bed. It starts again. I get back up. It stops. Nothing. I go back
> to bed. It rains. Hard. I sleep.
>
> *(Independent)*

But in the hands of an economical writer brief sentences can achieve a
satisfying rhythm:

> Romey's last hurrah was over in fifteen minutes. There were no tears.
> Even his secretary kept her composure. His daughter was not present.
> Very sad. He lived forty-four years and no one cried at his funeral.
>
> *(John Grisham)*

⇨ (See also FULL STOP)

SHALL / WILL

The difference between these two verb forms is generally side-stepped now,
either by the colloquial shortening to *'ll* (I'll, she'll), which buries the
difference, or by simply using *will* across the board. The somewhat
old-fashioned distinction between the two is that *shall* 'should' be used with
the first person singular and plural (I / we) and *will* with the second and third
persons, when all that is being expressed is simple futurity:

I / we shall see you tomorrow.

You / he / she / they will be at the station at 5.30.

The *shall / will* link with particular pronouns is reversed when the sentence
contains an element of compulsion, intention, determination: in short, anything
that makes it more than a simple statement about the future. In these cases the
first person (I / we) takes *will* while the others are followed by *shall*.

"I will do it, and there's no way you can stop me!"

"You shall go to the ball, Cinderella," said the fairy godmother.

In practice these fairly subtle distinctions are no longer observed, although
most people would register that the second example above is more forceful
than **"You will go to the ball...".**

⇨ (See also SHOULD / WOULD below)

SHOULD / WOULD

The difference between these two verb forms follows that for shall / will (*see
above*). *Should* can be used for the first person singular or plural:

I / we should like to thank the speaker.

while *would* is appropriate for other pronouns:

You / he / she / they would have arrived by now but for the snow.

The tendency is to use *would* in all cases (I / we would like to...) and the
formulation with *should* now sounds a little formal, which may be appropriate
in some contexts.

Should should, of course, be used with all pronouns when the meaning of
'ought to' is intended:

You really should try and see it.

SIBLING

A *sibling* is <u>someone who shares a parent with another</u>. 'Have you any
siblings?' means 'Have you any brothers or sisters?' The word is restricted to
written and official rather than spoken English, although it is an economical
term (four words rather than six in the sentences just quoted). *Sibling* has no
additional meaning. Here the writer presumably confused *sibling* with
'stripling', i.e. a young person:

✘✘ Colin Montgomerie was a sibling when he attended his first Ryder Cup match.

(Independent)

SLANG

'Slang' describes the English words that haven't yet sidled their way into respectability. On the spectrum it lies on the far side of the language termed 'colloquial' or 'conversational', which is itself beyond the band of English known as 'formal'. But there are grey areas – if one can have such things on a spectrum – lying between 'slang' and 'colloquial' and 'formal'. Language is never fixed. Yesterday's slang expression may be accepted with open arms in the language of today. For instance, <u>mob</u> was once objected to as slang, or a vulgarism, on the grounds that it was a shortened version of the phrase <u>mobile vulgus</u> (Latin for 'excitable crowd') – rather as today's formal English would reject 'ad' when used for 'advertisement'. Not all slang makes the grade and becomes accepted, however, and many words or phrases that were once in vogue have died away without establishing themselves in mainstream English. Nothing, it seems, dates more quickly than slang.

> **"Yessir. I seemed to be getting a lot of steam behind the punch. Well, I'm much obliged. I got those two bozoes a couple of beauts! You'd ought to have seen it. Bam... Wham!... and down they went. I near died laughing."**
>
> **It seemed to me it was time to squelch this kid. Too bally exuberant altogether...**
>
> **I spoke with considerable acerbity.**
>
> **"Well, you've gone and landed yourself in a nice posish. A dashed nice posish, I don't think."**
>
> *(P.G.Wodehouse)*

The language of such a piece at once places it in the first half of the twentieth century.

APPROPRIATENESS OF SLANG

The use of slang depends on audience and context. Some topics – sport or show business, for example – invite a slangy, non-formal approach. But slang is not for all men and women, or for all seasons. Some years ago Chris Patten, then the Conservative Party Chairman, was widely mocked when he claimed to be 'gobsmacked' by something or other. This was seen as an attempt, none too convincing, to enhance his street-cred (slang) by using a word that would not have sprung naturally to his lips. In 1995, Will Carling, the England captain, was (temporarily) stripped of his captaincy for calling the committee of the Rugby Football Union a collection of 'old farts'. It wasn't the idea so much as the expression that caused a rumpus. A phrase that would have been acceptable, maybe more than acceptable, with his team-mates or in bars up and down the country suddenly became dangerously offensive when uttered during a television documentary. If Carling had been more diplomatic and said something about the committee being 'a little out of touch', it is very unlikely that his words would have caused much of a stir. As it is, his remark served as a reminder of just how powerful slang can be, particularly when it occurs in an unexpected or inappropriate context.

Context and audience matter. We have different expectations of different speakers. We would be surprised by a judge in a bribery case talking of 'bungs' or of being 'well busy' or 'monster stunned', but this is very much what we would expect to hear from a football agent during an interview.

In speech there are no firm rules. Instead there is the much more intangible business of convention and the 'register' of speech, the right tone of voice for a particular occasion. Everybody uses some form of slang at some time (OK?), and many people, consciously or otherwise, adjust their quota of slang words according to their subject-matter and their audience. But if there are no rules there are still questions of taste and sensitivity and appropriateness. A vicar who talked during a funeral service about the deceased having 'kicked the bucket' would soon be hearing from his bishop.

When it comes to writing, the same considerations of appropriateness apply. Who is your audience? What is the occasion? What tone would be best? In imaginative writing, of course, there really are no rules. Slang adds enormously to the flavour and vigour of fiction. In 'factual' prose, whether a business letter, a Government White Paper, a newspaper article, it's a different story. English is, or is supposed to be on its best behaviour. Slang is outlawed. But it all depends...

Some newspapers make a practice of employing slang and colloquial English across the board. The _Sun_ has lead the way with its cast of 'oldies', 'fat cats', 'ciggies', 'hols', 'willies', and 'mums-of-six' with their 'tots'. The language would be out of place in a _Times_ editorial. Audience is the crucial consideration. But even the broadsheet papers make a distinction between the comparative soberness of their news reporting and the lighter note struck by feature articles, particularly if the topic wasn't too serious to begin with:

Covert soccer deals are done in this kind of place and here, I imagine, was the manager of some struggling team in the Stoby's World of Ice Freezer League waiting for a meet at which he'd offload some veteran midfield yob to a similar manager and receive a two-figure bung.

(from a restaurant review by Jonathan Meades, The Times)

If you are infatuated with your partner you don't give a fig for the rest of the world: if you fancy a quick game of tonsil tennis while you're waiting at the bus stop, what do you care if some old granny tuts disapprovingly and the bloke in the pinstripe suit doesn't know where to look.

(Anna Maxted, Independent)

In such passages the writers' pleasure in the slang is obvious, and the use of language almost becomes an end in itself. There are some areas where slang is off-limits, though. You will not read a company report which begins: 'ICI has enjoyed a stonking good year. The chairman is well happy...'

SLANG SOURCES
Slang derives from various sources.

Shortened words: circs; max; ciggie; offie (off-licence); boyf(riend)

Abbreviations: OTT (over the top); snafu (= chaos; from the initial letters of 'situation normal: all fucked [or fouled] up'.); sweet FA (= nothing whatsoever; from 'sweet Fanny Adams' or alternatively 'sweet fuck all').

Rhyming slang: butcher's (= look, from butcher's hook); iron hoof (= poof = male homosexual); north and south (= mouth).

Specialist slang is linked to jargon and argot, and describes the expressions used within a group, some of which may eventually spill over into mainstream use. Examples are given below of specialist slang within the Royal Navy:

fish	torpedo
gougher	big wave
lose the bubble	lose track, literally or metaphorically (when the bubble on the inclinometer in a submarine disappears you have lost control of the vessel)
sandscratchers	RN officers on surface ship (from submariners' viewpoint)
target	any surface ship (and not just enemy) to a submariner
vasco	navigator

SPASMODIC / SPORADIC

Spasmodic means <u>happening by fits and starts</u>:

> **The engine wouldn't start though it made spasmodic efforts to burst into life.**

Sporadic means <u>scattered</u>, <u>occurring in no fixed pattern</u>:

> **Headlights were small and sporadic along the distant highway.**
>
> *(Patricia Cornwell, The Body Farm)*

It is hard to distinguish between these two adjectives although *spasmodic* suggests a measure of jerkiness or violence.

SPECIAL / ESPECIAL

⇨ See ESPECIAL / SPECIAL

SPECIALITY / SPECIALTY

The two nouns mean exactly the same, a <u>particular skill or product</u> (e.g. the dish that a restaurant prides itself on). *Speciality* is the British English spelling while *specialty* is essentially US, if creeping into British usage.

SPLIT INFINITIVE

For pedantic grammarians the most memorable moment in the TV series <u>Star Trek</u> was the voice-over at the beginning announcing that the Starship *Enterprise* and her crew were about 'to boldly go' into the realms of unexplored space. 'To boldly go' is a split infinitive.

The present infinitive form of a verb – **to hope, to work, to go** – is split when an adverb or adverbial phrase is inserted between the two words: **to earnestly hope**; **to first of all work**; **to boldly go**. There are no grammatical grounds for objecting to split infinitives, and while one should not go out one's way <u>to deliberately separate</u> **to** from its parent verb there is no need <u>to studiously avoid</u> the splits. Of the five examples of the split infinitive in the last two sentences, only **to first of all work** might be better avoided. It has a slightly cumbersome sound. Sometimes the infinitive has to be split so as to convey the writer's meaning precisely. **They hoped privately to influence the Prime Minister** is different from **They hoped to privately influence the Prime Minister**. (**Privately** qualifies **hoped** in the first sentence but **influence** in the second.) Many writers happily split their infinitives, and the heavens do not fall:

> **...to trudge along for miles in order to never quite be able to hear a speech from Tony Benn ...**
>
> *(Guardian)*
>
> **In some ways it is 'cred' to still live with your mum...**
>
> *(Daily Telegraph)*
>
> **The company now has exciting plans to dramatically expand...**
>
> *(The Times)*

STATIONARY / ERY

Stationary (adjective only) means <u>not moving</u>:

> **... I puzzle over a large group riding one-wheel stationary bikes ...**
>
> *(The Times)*

Stationery (noun only) is what is bought from a station<u>er</u>'s.

STRAIGHT / STRAIT

The adjective *straight* means <u>direct, without a curve</u>. The noun use is mostly found in a racing context:

> **The favourite was ahead all the way down the final straight.**

Strait is an obsolete adjective meaning <u>narrow, confining</u> (only found now in *straitjacket* and *straitlaced)*. As a noun, usually in the plural, *strait(s)* describes <u>a narrow stretch of water between two seas</u> (**Straits of Gibraltar; Bass Strait**) or has the sense of <u>difficult circumstances</u>:

After the house sale fell through they found themselves in dire financial straits.

STRATUM / STRATA

Stratum, meaning <u>layer</u> or <u>level</u>, is the singular noun form; *strata* is the plural:

In this stratum of society... / Examination of these rock strata...

⇨ (See also CRITERION / A)

SUBSTANTIAL / SUBSTANTIVE

Substantial means <u>solid</u>, <u>large</u>:

She was left a substantial amount of money.

Substantive also has something of the sense of <u>solid</u> but not with a physical application. The adjective is increasingly popular in the context of diplomacy, pay negotiations, and so on, where it has the meaning of <u>firm</u>, <u>achieving something worthwhile</u>:

The heads of state were unwilling to meet unless they felt that substantive progress could be made towards peace.

SUPERIOR / INFERIOR

Superior and *inferior*, meaning <u>better</u> and <u>worse</u> respectively, are already in comparative form. Therefore it is incorrect – and repetitive – to talk of something being 'more superior' or 'less inferior':

✘ **'... claims that privatisation would lead to a more inferior service.'**
   (quoted, Radio 4)

SUPINE

⇨ See PRONE

TAUTOLOGY

Tautology is using too many words to say the same thing:

'We ask people to be short, brief and to the point.'
   (Radio 4)

It's hard to avoid tautology in speech, and often this kind of repetition is an entirely justified method of providing emphasis in both spoken and written English:

There was no way out, no exit, no escape.

However, the use of certain adjectives to describe nouns gives a more obvious example of redundant language:

well-informed expert

safe haven

dreadful outrage

future predictions

emotional feeling

rough approximation

> *(the information provided by the adjective is already contained in the noun, by definition.)*

In the following examples the unnecessary word or phrase is underlined:

> **... her assertion that harassment of her by railwaymen was not treated <u>equally</u> as seriously.**
>
> *(The Times)*

[**as** could be removed instead of **equally**]

> **... practices which are illegal outside <u>of</u> prison should not be permitted on the inside...**
>
> *(Telegraph)*

The <u>close</u> proximity of the Air Ministry ...

> *(The Times)*

> **... an extraordinary new world, to which <u>past</u> history offers the guide.**
>
> *(Guardian)*

She was flanked by two women prison officers, <u>one on either side</u>.

> *(Radio 4)*

⇨ (See REPETITION)

TEMERITY / TIMIDITY

Temerity means <u>daring</u>, with the suggestion of rashness. It is more usually applied to, say, challenges to authority, than cases of physical daring:

> **The defendant had the temerity to question the sanity of the judge in open court.**

Timidity points to an opposite attitude: <u>lack of nerve</u>, a shyness that makes its possessor unassertive:

> **Timidity made him reluctant to speak out even when his own interests were being threatened.**

TEMPORARY / TEMPORAL

Both adjectives are connected to time, and are occasionally confused.
Temporary means <u>for a (short) time only</u>:

His temporary work lasted only until August.

Temporal means <u>related to time,</u> <u>of this world</u> (as opposed to 'spiritual'), and is properly applied in fairly rare contexts. The lords *temporal* are those members of the House of Lords who are lay peers (i.e. not bishops).

THANKFULLY

Thankfully means <u>gratefully</u>:

They had been waiting for rain and sighed thankfully as the first drops fell.

However, *thankfully* is more often used in the sense of <u>it is something to be thankful for that,</u> and is generally acceptable in this sense:

Thankfully, the crash injured no one.

There is possible ambiguity where the adverb is linked to a personal pronoun:

Thankfully he pulled through after the crash.

and it is not immediately clear which of the two senses of *thankfully* is meant.

⇨ (See also HOPEFULLY, REGRETFUL / REGRETTABLE)

THAT / WHICH

That and *which* can be used interchangeably but only in cases where *which* is not preceded by a comma (i.e. only in defining clauses – *see WHICH / ,WHICH; WHO / ,WHO*).

The city firms that had been invited to tender for the work complained that they had been given too little time.

(but:

✗✗ The city firms, that had been invited to tender for the work, complained...

would be wrong.)

That is sometimes used simply for a variation on *which*:

... the British and French governments, which own the state railways that in turn own Eurostar ...

(The Times)

THEIR / THERE / THEY'RE

Their is the possessive form of the pronoun *they*:

They wanted the cash to prop up their collapsing empire...

(Sun)

There is an adverb of place (**over there**) or used to start a sentence or introduce certain verbs (especially 'to be'):

"**There were moments when we were in real trouble.**"

(Sun)

They're is the elided or contracted form of *they are*, and should be used only in informal contexts:

"**They're sick as parrots over the 10-0 defeat.**"

TITLES

The titles of books, plays, songs, films, newspapers, etc. should be distinguished from the body of the text in which they are mentioned. The minimum requirement is to capitalise the principal words in the title:

Coronation Street

Lord of the Flies

Whatever Happened to the Likely Lads?

Only connecting words like 'and', 'of', 'to' do not require capitalising, and there is a play-safe tendency to capitalise all words now.

The convention in printing is to italicise titles as well as using capitals:

the TV series *Happy Days*

John Wayne's last film, *The Shootist*

(the handwritten equivalent is to underline the title)

Not marking off a title in some way may cause ambiguity. Macbeth is a character in Shakespeare's play; the play is titled *Macbeth*. Apollo 13 was a space flight launched in 1970; *Apollo 13*, a film about the flight, was released in 1995.

Another convention is to use italicisation or underlining for long titles but single quotation marks for short stories, poems and songs.

Dickens's short story 'The Signalman'; his novel *Bleak House*.

Current practice, however, tends to set all titles in italic, irrespective of length:

...the harmonic octaves of *Oh my blacke Soule*.

...a gentle, yearning number called *Can't Get You Off My Mind*...

(The Times)

In this book, because of the number of different type styles used in each entry, we have set titles and newspaper names in italic and underlined.

Ships' names are usually italicised in print: **Nelson's *Victory*.**

Newspaper titles should also be italicised / underlined, with *The Times* being distinguished from the rest of the press by having the definite article included (compare the *Sun*, the *Telegraph*).

⇨ (See also CAPITALS, QUOTATION MARKS)

TO / TOO

To signifies the infinitive form of a verb or is used as a link word (preposition):

[The BBC] **paid £1.2 million to lure Chris to the station ...**
(Sun)

Too, meaning <u>in addition</u> (**and the dog came too**) or <u>in excess</u> (**too much**), is an adverb.

TORPID / TORRID

Torpid (adjective) means <u>sluggish</u>:
The hot weather made the animals torpid.

Torrid (adjective) means <u>scorching</u>, <u>parched</u>:
The torrid climate meant we couldn't go out during the day.

(The most usual application of *torrid* is in its associated sense of 'hot with passion', and the word joins the honourable little roll-call of terms that signal sexual content in a film, play, etc. Others include 'sensual', 'explicit', 'frank', and the ever-popular 'steamy'.)

TORTUOUS / TORTUROUS

Tortuous (an adjective) means <u>twisting</u> or <u>highly complicated</u>:
We almost got lost on the tortuous mountain path.

Torturous (adjective) derives from *torture*, and means <u>causing severe physical or mental pain</u>:
I spent a torturous hour jammed in the tiny one-man canoe.

Both words could be applied to the same thing. Becoming involved in a legal process, for example, might be a *tortuous* and a *torturous* experience. However, they have distinct meanings and should not be confused.

TRIUMPHANT / TRIUMPHAL(IST)

Triumphant means <u>rejoicing in victory</u>, and generally applies to individuals, teams, etc., and their words and behaviour after they've won:
The team was triumphant after their fifth victory in a row.

Triumphal describes rather the process of <u>commemorating a victory</u>.

So an arch or a column – or a march – could be *triumphal*.

Recently popular is the adjective *triumphalist*, suggesting <u>gloating in victory</u>, and a forgetting of the cost of that victory:
'The commemoration of the end of the [Second World] **War is not a triumphalist occasion.'**
(John Major, House of Commons)

TRY AND / TRY TO

Try and is used very widely in speech and informal contexts:
I'll try and get to see it if I can.

Try to is better English, and should be used in formal contexts:

The committee has tried to improve facilities for members.

TURBID / TURGID

Turbid means <u>confused</u> or <u>muddy</u>:

The water was turbid from the landslides that had occurred upriver.

The more frequently used adjective *turgid* means <u>swollen</u>, <u>pompous</u>, and is often applied to a writer or speaker's prose style:

The report was stuffed with turgid statements from the chairman about the company's wonderful prospects.

UNATTACHED PARTICIPLES & DANGLERS

A descriptive phrase used at the start of a sentence and followed by a comma will attach itself to the nearest noun or pronoun which comes afterwards.

Like many a highly strung young dealer, he went on drinking sprees with colleagues.

(Independent on Sunday)

Cornered, one blames St Paul.

(The Times)

If the phrase is linked to the 'wrong' following word the sense of the sentence may not be obscured but the meaning is not strictly what the writer intended, and may have comic overtones:

✘ **Shot entirely at sea of Hawaii, director Kevin Reynolds developed seasickness, while cameramen complained about the constant bobbing up and down.**

(Guardian)

(the director was shot entirely at sea)

✘ **Loosely based on a Phillip K Dick story, construction worker Arnold Schwarzenegger finds his memory has been erased...**

(Independent)

(Arnold Scharzenegger is loosely based on a Philip K Dick story)

✘ **After the first day, sleeping after a 1,000ft climb, my underpants were eaten by warrior ants.**

(The Times)

(his underpants were fast asleep)

✘ **Joining initially as Partner Designate, we will offer you a clearly defined short-term path ...**

(recruitment advertisement)

(Who's doing the joining here? It sounds like us but it should be the 'you' the advertisement is directed at. **Joining initially as Partner Designate, you will be offered...**)

When the introductory phrase contains a participle form of a verb ('cornered', 'joining') and is attached to the wrong word, the mistake is termed an unattached participle. Where the participle does not relate to anything at all it is called a dangling participle:

> **Glancing through their results, it seemed a long time since they had won a match.**

(Who is glancing here?)

UNDERSTATEMENT

Understatement, the playing down or modest treatment of a topic, is a very common feature of spoken English: 'Not bad' and 'Pretty good' both mean something between 'good' and 'very good'; while 'Not too good' means anything between 'bad' and 'very bad'. Similarly 'Quite a lot' indicates a large quantity; and 'Spot of bother' and 'Bit of a scrap' may be applied to a military engagement or even a full-scale battle.

In written English *understatement* emerges in the *not un-* formula: not unhopeful; not unattractive. And there is an innate tendency in many people to use qualifiers such as 'quite', 'fairly', 'moderately'.

Used moderately (!), *understatement* can be a useful way of drawing distinctions: there is a difference between "I am hopeful" and "I am not unhopeful".

⇨ (See also EXAGGERATION)

UNDERTONE

⇨ See OVERTONE

UNINTERESTED

⇨ See DISINTERESTED

UNIQUE

More (or *most*) *unique* is disliked on the grounds that if something is *unique* there is nothing else like it in the world – and therefore it can't be the subject of a comparison:

✗ **The Taj Mahal is more unique than the Eiffel Tower.**

✗ **'Advertisers in the US are finding the hotel guest a very unique target.'**

> *(quoted, Independent on Sunday)*

On the other hand you can claim that something approaches the state of uniqueness, since a number of things can be in that position:

This commercial advantage is almost unique to media products ...

(Independent on Sunday)

(*Unique* should not be used when 'exceptional' is meant:

✗ Pele was unique football player and so were Cruyff and Maradona.)

UP TO

⇨ See DOWN TO

USE / UTILISE

Utilise suggests an active putting to use of whatever one can find:

Robinson Crusoe utilised the resources of his desert island.

Use is a plainer term:

He used his knowledge of languages to get by.

Utilise is sometimes used because *use* doesn't sound sufficiently important (rather as some people prefer to commence instead of start). But the shorter word is usually good enough.

VERACITY / VORACITY

Veracity is truthfulness:

The veracity of stories about King Arthur is very doubtful.

Voracity is greed (usually in eating):

The guests set on the the buffet with a voracity I'd never seen before.

(The more familiar adjectival form is *voracious*. The adjective from *veracity* is *veracious*.)

VERB

A verb is traditionally defined as a 'doing' word and while this is a clichéd and inadequate description it is hard to produce a short, comprehensible definition that will not do an even worse job than 'doing'. Verbs are the most vital parts of sentences; without them sentences wouldn't be sentences; but a single verb can compose a sentence all by itself – Help! Stop! Think! (Further discussion of verbs will be found in the Glossary, *page 187*.)

ACTIVE OR PASSIVE?

The difference between the active and passive voice is simply illustrated by the following:

(Active) **He kicked the ball.**

(Passive) **The ball was kicked by him.**

The active voice is generally recommended by writers on style. Or to put in another way – the active way – writers on style generally recommend the active voice. An active construction usually looks simpler and more direct than the passive construction. A simple sentence such as **She took the decision to go** places the subject of the sentence right next to what she did, puts 'her' in charge as it were. If the sentence is converted to the passive voice, **The decision to go was taken by her**, the sense remains the same but there is a slight muffling of the clarity of the first version (which is also two words shorter), as well as a subtle diminution of 'her' capacity in decision-making.

For this reason, bureaucratic documents, minutes, reports and so on often use an impersonal, passive formulation.

> **This matter was considered by the board ...**

> **It was felt that ...**

> **A decision was eventually reached ...**

A kind of baffle is inserted between the thing that was done and the human beings who did it. A collective noun like 'board' or 'committee' smooths away individual responsibility, while phrasing that employs the passive voice makes for a further reduction in the human share. In certain areas this is almost inevitable; legal phraseology produces plenty of passive expressions:

> **The slip rule could be relied on to correct an order where the form of the order reflected the form of the Official Receiver's summons and was sought to be corrected on the ground that an error of law was made when its terms were agreed between counsel and passed and entered by the court.**

> *(Law report)*

As a general rule, and in everyday non-specialist writing, one should avoid a run of passives or at least vary them with sentences that use the active construction. There are, however, occasions when it is difficult to avoid the passive. For example, the sentence 'The cat was run over last week' can only be turned into an active construction if the speaker knows who or what ran over the cat, or uses an all-purpose noun like 'somebody'.

IRREGULAR VERBS

A number of English verbs do not follow the pattern of adding *-ed* in the past tense or past participle form which is standard for the great majority: chop / chopped, offer / offered. A few examples follow:

infinitive	*past tense*	*past participle*	
bear	born(e)	born(e)	(see separate entry)
burn	burned / burnt	burned / burnt	(either form can be used)
dream	dreamed / dreamt	dreamed / dreamt	(either form)

drink	drank	drunk	('drunk' now rare as past tense)
hang	hanged / hung	hanged / hung	(see separate entry)
leap	leaped / leapt	leaped / leapt	(either form)
learn	learned / learnt	learned / learnt	(either form)
lie	lay / laid	laid / lain	(see separate entry)
light	lighted / lit	lighted / lit	(either form)
shrink	shrank	shrunk	(sometimes 'shrunk' in past tense)
sing	sang	sung	('sung' now rare as past tense)
smell	smelled / smelt	smelled / smelt	(either form)
spell	spelled / spelt	spelled / spelt	(either form)
spill	spilled / spilt	spilled / spilt	(either form)
thrive	throve	thriven	(but now more likely to be 'thrived' for past tense and participle)

VERBS INTO NOUNS

The more usual process is for nouns to be turned into verbs but the trade can work in the opposite direction, particularly in the fields of business and advertising. If the words are newly used in this way they may strike an incongruous note:

> **According to Northern... that is a serious <u>undervalue</u> of the rump ...**
>
> *(Independent)*

Spend and *take* (in the sense of a 'snapshot' exposing attitude) are buzzword nouns at the moment, as well as being workhorse verbs:

> **Enigma's marketing spend this year will be £8 million.**
>
> *(The Times)*

> **.... the whole a fascinating take on America by an English ad agency working for a Turin rubber company.**
>
> *(Independent on Sunday)*

WHICH / THAT

⇨ See THAT / WHICH

WHICH / ,WHICH

The difference between *which* without a preceding comma and *,which* (with the comma) is the difference between a defining and a descriptive clause respectively. The following sentences are identical except for the placing of the commas:

The painting which was in the attic was valued at £5000.

(This was the attic painting; the place where it was found defines it. The implication of the sentence is that there were other paintings elsewhere which were less – or more – valuable. So the next sentence might go: 'But the one in the cellar was worth £10000.')

When commas are introduced the meaning is different:

The painting, which was in the attic, was valued at £5000.

(Here the clause introduced by *which* is simply descriptive. The painting happened to be in the attic, rather than somewhere else.)

⇨ (see also WHO / ,WHO)

WHILE / WHILST

These two words mean exactly the same thing, but *whilst* has a slightly fussy, pursed-lips quality to it. What's wrong with *while* ? The writer of this example hedged her bets by using both *while* and *whilst* in the space of a couple of lines:

Research... found that whilst 63 per cent of female students were very or quite sympathetic to feminism, just over half made negative remarks about feminists. Thus while many young women are feminist in all but name ...

(Independent)

WHO / ,WHO

The difference between *who* (without a preceding comma) and *,who* (with a comma) is that the first introduces a defining clause and the second a descriptive one. Compare:

a) **The men who were in their twenties were ordered to report for duty the following day.**

with

b) **The men, who were in their twenties, were ordered to report for duty the following day.**

The first – defining – example of *who* (a) indicates that only those in their 20s (and no other age group) had to report. The second – descriptive – use of,who (b) tells us that the men happened to be in their 20s, but doesn't suggest that their age was necessarily a factor in what they were required to do. In the first sentence the men's age is all-important; in the second it's an incidental detail.

In the following example (from a notice on a packet):

✘ **Not suitable for small children who can choke on nuts**

the comma should have been placed before *who* since the warning is for all children, and not merely those who would choke. The 'who' clause should be descriptive, not defining.

It's sometimes hard to decide whether a clause is defining or descriptive. The writer of the following has hedged his or her bets:

✗ Mary is a cleaner, who cleans for Leila who is a university lecturer, who is writing a book about Becky.

(The Times)

(Commas should have been used uniformly [ie, between *Leila* and *who*] or should have been left out altogether. The sentence also shows that repeated use of *who*, whether intended to be humorous or not, is usually confusing. The reader has to refer back to find out who is the subject of this particular *who*.)

⇨ (see also WHICH / ,WHICH)

WHO / WHOM

Enter the *who / whom* debate and you enter a little minefield of anxiety. The gap between correct usage and what generally happens is wide. It may be true, as some linguistic prophets claim, that *whom* is on the way out. But if it is about to become as redundant as the human appendix it is still capable of flaring up and causing trouble, just like that anatomical anachronism.

Absolute correctness requires the consistent use of *who* as the subject of a verb and *whom* as the object of a verb or following from a preposition:

In the show it is Gayle King, her best friend, to whom she once gave a million dollars for a Christmas present, who stands in as her sister.

(The Times)

(*whom* is the object of 'gave'; *who* the subject of 'stands')

It is normal to find *who* in speech rather than the technically correct *whom*:

'I'm becoming – definitely have become – as interested in who I work with as what I work on.'

(quoted, Independent on Sunday)

(Indeed, being 'right' in speech can sound stilted and unnatural:

'Whom are you going to allow to finance it?'

[quoted, Independent on Sunday])

The general use of *who*, when *whom* would be gramatically correct, is increasingly common in writing:

When our partners, who we've sworn never to leave..

(The Times)

... a respected House historian who Mr Gingrich had summarily dismissed after 12 years' service ...

(The Times)

And a large *Guardian* headline (over an article on factory farming) – **Who's** killing who? — almost certainly opted for the 'wrong' form of the word to avoid the slight fussiness that can sometimes be suggested by *whom*.

Using *who* when it is the direct object of a verb (as in the last three examples) is more acceptable than keeping the word unchanged when it follows a preposition. Here convention favours the switch to *whom*:

> ... he started with no preconceptions about Mountbatten, about whom he knew little ...
>
> *(The Times)*

although it is not hard to find cases that don't follow convention, particularly where the writer is aiming at a conversational tone:

> ... since she minds enough about who you sleep with to want it to be her, exclusively, and for good ...
>
> *(GQ)*

THE WRONG WHOM

It's easy to go wrong in the other direction and put down *whom* because the construction of the sentence makes it look as though the object form of the word is correct. This tends to occur after verbs like 'think' or 'believe', as in the following examples:

✗✗ ... the 27-year-old whom the US authorities believe carried out the bombing.

> *(Independent)*

✗✗ The other's from unmarried friends from way back, whom we thought were like us (happily unmarried, but bound by a clutch of deliberate offspring) ...

> *(Independent)*

✗✗ Meanwhile GPs, whom the Government assumed were eager to take on hospital work such as small operations, are giving warnings ...

> *(Independent on Sunday)*

In each case *whom* is the subject of a verb, and not the object of one, and therefore *who* should be used:

> ... the 27-year-old who... carried out the bombing ...
>
> *(subject of 'carried')*

> ... unmarried friends... who... were like us ...
>
> *(subject of 'were')*

> ... GPs, who... were eager ...
>
> *(subject of 'were')*

The simplest way to establish which form is correct is to recast the subordinate clause as a separate sentence – 'The US authorities believe that he...'; 'The

Government assumed that they...'. Using 'he' and 'they' indicates that 'who' is right.

The following show how it should be done:

Kathy Mitchell... the one who brush salesmen always hope will open the door ...

(Guardian)

...Czech model Adriana Sklemarikova, who pals said he was set to wed.

(Sun)

WHO / WHICH

Who is used for individuals:

The man who broke the bank at Monte Carlo.

and *which* for events, objects, etc.:

The historic battle which took place on this spot.

Countries and human groups sometimes take *who*, and there is an indeterminate area where either *who* or *which* can be used:

Our products are inspired by other cultures who have used plants safely and effectively for centuries.

(Body Shop advert)

Similarly with animals: reference to an individual animal (particularly a pet) will probably be followed by *who*, but a collective noun (flock, herd) will take *which*.

WHO'S / WHOSE

Who's is the contracted form of *who is*. *Whose* is the possessive form of *who*. The words have an identical sound but completely different functions, neatly illustrated by this line from a play:

"Who's this old relic, whose side is he on?"

(quoted, The Times)

The usual mistake is to put the contracted form in the place of the possessive:

✗✗ The Icelandic pop pixie [Bjork], who's new single, Army Of Me, soared into the Top Ten last week ...

(Daily Star)

✗✗ ... they too demand to know on who's side he will be fighting.

(The Times)

WILL

⇨ See SHALL

WOMANISH / WOMANLY

Neither adjective is very often found. *Womanish* means <u>effeminate</u>, and would therefore be used to describe a man.

Womanly means <u>feminine</u>.

⇨ (See also CHILDISH / CHILDLIKE, MACHO / MANLY / MANNISH)

WOULD

⇨ See SHOULD

GLOSSARY

ACTIVE CONSTRUCTION

The *active* construction of a sentence is one in which the subject carries out the
action decribed by the verb:

I painted the room.

>*(subject: I; verb: painted)*

**The correspondent described the horrendous conditions in the
country.**

>*(subject: correspondent; verb: described)*

>*(A passive construction turns things round: **The room was painted by
me**)*

⇨ (See also PASSIVE in *Glossary*, and VERB in main section for discussion of
stylistic differences between active and passive.)

ADJECTIVE *(Part of speech)*

Adjectives give additional information about a noun or a pronoun. They
are to do with colour, size, shape, age, frequency, mood, etc.

<u>Worried</u> wife Jean Brown goes to bed <u>every</u> night in her <u>new</u> Skoda.

...he was <u>desperate</u> to hit the <u>local</u> night-spots.

>*(Daily Star)*

⇨ (See also COMPARATIVE and SUPERLATIVE)

ADVERB *(Part of speech)*

Like adjectives, *adverbs* play a supporting role in speech. They convey
information about how an action is performed, they indicate place or time, they
modify adjectives:

'To travel <u>hopefully</u> is better than to arrive...'

>*(Robert Louis Stevenson)*

On her first long drive she got <u>uncomfortably</u> sunburned.

>*(The Times)*

**"... including Pamela, who was <u>really</u> nervous about not wearing eye
make-up..."**

>*(quoted, Sun)*

Most adverbs can be identified by their -ly endings (efficient<u>ly</u>, gradual<u>ly</u>,
deep<u>ly</u>), but there are plenty of exceptions, among them some of the most
familiar words:

The bright green spears of English asparagus are best taken <u>straight</u> from market to pan

(<u>Guardian</u>)

He's <u>still</u> the same as he <u>ever</u> was.

ALLITERATION

Alliteration is using the same letter(s) at the start of a series of words. Alliteration is used intentionally in advertising (**Double Diamond Works Wonders** was a long-running campaign) and in poetry:

And still she slept an azure-lidded sleep,

In blanched linen, smooth, and lavender'd ...

(Keats)

Alliteration is often without any function; the writer merely likes the sound of a sequence of words with the same initial letter:

... the Tory chairman... had gathered his grey and gaunt gaggle of loyalists ...

(<u>The Times</u>)

APOSTROPHE *(Punctuation)*

The *apostrophe* has two uses:

a) to show possession:

the judge's summing-up

the dog's dinner

Bill's house

b) to indicate where letters have dropped out of words:

there's

shouldn't

12 o'clock

The apostrophe causes problems, perhaps more so than any other single piece of punctuation.

⇨ See APOSTROPHE in main section for further discussion.

BRACKETS

⇨ See PARENTHESIS in *Glossary*

CLAUSE

A *clause* is a set of words which includes a finite verb.

⇨ See MAIN CLAUSE and SUBORDINATE CLAUSE for definition of the two types of clause.

COLLOQUIAL ENGLISH

Colloquial English is the term for the language as it is spoken and as it appears in more informal writing. It is hard to discriminate with any exactness between standard and *colloquial* English, and between *colloquial* and slang. The borders are not fixed, and terms which started out in the lowly realms of slang and *colloquialism* have a habit of creeping their way into respectability.

As some sort of indication of the difference, take the colloqual sentence:

> **My dad asked me whether it was OK to go in the motor now or whether he'd still be risking his neck.**

Put into standard English this would become something like:

> **My father asked me whether it was safe to drive in the car now or whether he would still be putting himself in danger by doing so.**

Choosing between *colloquial* and standard English depends entirely on the context the language is to be used in. Formal occasions – writing application letters for jobs, for example – demand a formal approach. Much of the time, however, *colloquial* English is appropriate and often, as the example above indicates, more vigorous than standard English.

⇨ (See STANDARD ENGLISH in *Glossary*)

⇨ (See LETTER WRITING and SLANG in the main section)

COLON *(Punctuation)*

The *colon* signals a break between the segments of a sentence which it separates. It is a stronger piece of punctuation than the comma. The comonest use of the *colon* is to signal that what comes after it is an explanation or amplification of a preceding statement:

> **From Karachi to the Khyber, he [Imran Khan] is a god in many incarnations: cricket idol, pin-up, playboy, political dabbler, champion of the poor.**
>
> *(The Times)*

The *colon* is frequently used to announce that what follows is a series of examples – as in this book.

⇨ (See COLON in main section)

COMMA *(Punctuation)*

The *comma* is the briefest form of punctuation, and its use is, very roughly, equivalent to those places where a speaker would pause:

> **Sales of hosepipes, electric fans, ice-cream, beer and sun-screen are, of course, booming as they do every time the British sun comes out.**
>
> *(Independent on Sunday)*

The (quite complicated) rules for the use of the *comma* are discussed in COMMA in main section.

COMPARATIVE (ADJECTIVE)

The *comparative* form of the adjective should be used when two things are being compared. It should not be used if three or more things are referred to. Almost all adjectives can be put in the comparative form by the addition of '-er' at the end of the word or the addition of 'more' in front of it:

brighter

plainer

more frightening

more intelligent

⇨ (See also SUPERLATIVE)

COMPOUND ADJECTIVE

A *compound adjective* is formed by joining two (or more) adjectives together or a noun and an adjective:

blue-grey

bitter-sweet

self-seeking

head-hunting

long-sighted

full-blooded

CONJUNCTION *(Part of speech)*

Conjunctions are link words like **and, but, where, either, or, although**. The operate as the glue or mortar in a sentence.

A *co-ordinating conjunction* brings together two words or groups of words which are gramatically equivalent:

My husband <u>and</u> I...

Don't drink <u>and</u> drive.

To be <u>or</u> not to be...

He's a fine actor <u>but</u> he's also a star face.

What is being said on each side of the conjunction has an equal significance or weight.

A *subordinating conjunction* introduces a subordinate clause, a group of words whose full interpretation depends on a main clause (*see* MAIN and SUBORDINATE CLAUSE):

"He was a rotten looking Santa anyway <u>because</u> he had a mean grumpy face."

(quoted, <u>Sun</u>)

Don't count your chickens <u>until</u> they're hatched.

The application of the words following **because, until** rests on the main clauses that come first. A subordinating conjunction can be used to start a sentence – **<u>If</u> you want to know the time ask a policeman** – but the clause it introduces will still be dependent on the main clause.

DASH *(Punctuation)*

A single *dash* operates like a colon, separating two parts of a sentence. What comes after the *dash* often 'explains' what has preceded it:

'Quitting [smoking] is about doing something positive – proving you are a master of your own destiny.'

(quoted, Independent on Sunday)

Used in pairs *dashes* work like brackets (*see also* PARENTHESIS in main section and Glossary). They enclose an additional piece of information within the main body of the sentence:

... interesting how the top two movies – 'Citizen Kane' and 'The Godfather' – have so many concerns in common.

(Time Out)

After his shock decision to quit in 1976 – he broke the news to the Queen as she was washing up – Wilson returned to the backbenches.

(Sun)

⇨ (See DASH in main section)

DOTS *(Punctuation)*

Dots (elliptical dots to give them their full name) indicate that a portion of text has been missed out in a quoted passage. At the end of a paragraph they may indicate that time has passed before the events recounted in the next paragraph or, irrespective of placing, they suggest that whatever business, process or event is being described is in some way unfinished.

Little did they know what the night would bring...

is a heated example of this application of *elliptical dots*.

⇨ (See ELLIPICAL DOTS in main section)

EPONYM

An *eponym* is a person who gives his or her name to something. Thus the guillotine is named after the Frenchman Dr Guillotin (1738-1814) and the sandwich after the Earl of Sandwich (1718-92). Processes named after people are also *eponymous*. Milk which is pasteurised is sterilised because of the discoveries of Louis Pasteur (1822-95), while in the early nineteenth century Dr Bowdler (1754-1825) performed a service to families everywhere by producing a bowdlerised Shakespeare, an edition of the plays with all the rude and suggestive material expurgated. On the whole, words derived from individuals – boycott, sadism, cardigan – take a lower case letter, not a capital, at the beginning.

An *eponymous* hero / heroine is one who gives his / her name to a book, play, film, opera: Hamlet, Tess of the D'Urbervilles, Tosca.

EXCLAMATIONS / INTERJECTIONS *(Part of speech)*

Exclamations or *interjections* (sometimes called ejaculations) like **Oh** and **Ah!** and **er** are used all the time in spoken English. They count as marginal parts of speech. They express something – often a very strong something – but in themselves have no meaning.

⇨ (See EXCLAMATIONS in main section for use in written English)

EXCLAMATION MARK *(Punctuation)*

An *exclamation mark* denotes surprise, rage, indignation, decisiveness on the part of the speaker or writer – any strong response:

At least 50 people volunteered for this dangerous mission!

Used in the middle of a sentence, and usually bracketed (!), the *exclamation mark* suggests the author's doubt or perhaps ironic surprise at some fact or opinion he or she is passing on.

⇨ (See EXCLAMATION MARK in main section)

FIGURE OF SPEECH

A *figure of speech* is a term used to describe a metaphorical use of language, i.e. when words are not used in their literal sense. Phrases such as 'driving me up the wall', 'going for broke', 'right as rain', are *figures of speech*. The term can also be applied to exaggerated applications of language like 'There were millions of people in the room.'

Language used in this way can be termed *figurative*.

⇨ (See also METAPHOR, SIMILE and PERSONIFICATION in *Glossary*)

FINITE VERB

⇨ See VERB in the *Glossary*

FULL STOP *(Punctuation)*

A *full stop* signifies the end of a sentence:

He almost fell out of his chair in surprise.

Full stops are also used to signify abbreviations:

Co.; Pres.; Govt.; dept.; Min.; Rev.

The *full stop* dot also forms part of the symbols indicating question marks and exclamation marks, which function as *full stops* when placed at the end of sentences.

⇨ (See SENTENCE in *Glossary*, and ABBREVIATION, FULL STOP and SENTENCE in main section)

GERUND

The term *gerund*, derived from Latin, describes a very ordinary feature of the English language: a noun derived from a verb and ending in *-ing*, and therefore indistinguishable from the present participle (showing, running, thinking). Whether a particular *-ing* word is a present participle or a gerund depends on its position and function in a sentence:

We saw him as he was <u>running</u> across the common.

(participle)

Moderate <u>running</u> is supposed to be good for your health.

(gerund – running is the noun subject of the sentence)

GRAMMAR

Grammar is 'the science of language'. But *grammar* is also defined in the same dictionary (Chambers) as an art – the art of using the language in the right way (i.e. according to grammatical rules). If *grammar* is a science, it is not a very precise one. Most, if not all, of its laws can be broken (at least occasionally), and the language will still work. That is, it will still communicate. On the other hand, if *grammar* is an art, it is less in the sense in which painting and poetry-writing are arts and more in the sense in which carpentry can be described as an art. *Grammar* is to do with how the bits of language fit together, or how they may best be made to fit together – not by force, but with a little knowledge, patience and experimentation.

HYPHEN *(Punctuation)*

Hyphens are used to join two or more words together, or to separate a prefix from its parent word:

post-mortem

co-operate

free-range

back-pedal

re-elect

or to indicate that a word runs from one line to the next and has been broken because of limitations of space.

⇨ (See HYPHEN in main section)

IDIOM

An *idiom* is an expression which is figurative or metaphorical and which is less than the sum of its parts: 'on a hiding to nothing'; 'at sixes and sevens'; 'fly in the ointment'. Idioms are often particular to a language and not readily translatable. 'Peculiar', in fact, might be a better word than 'particular' as many idioms turn distinctly odd if one stops to think about them. Phrases like 'a chip off the old block', 'nutty as a fruitcake', 'be on cloud nine', 'once in a blue moon', 'a turn-up for the book', are readily understood by almost all native English speakers. But someone coming to the language from outside and with only a basic vocabulary would have difficulty interpreting what was meant by them, even though the words that make up each phrase are short and familiar. Almost all *idioms* are metaphorical, and although they have equivalents in other languages which express the same ideas they could not be translated precisely as they stand.

An *idiomatic* expression may be confined to a particular region of a country, and the adjective is occasionally applied to a single user who has his or her own manner of handling language.

⇨ (See CLICHÉ in main section)

INTRANSITIVE VERB

The principal distinction between verbs is between *transitive* and intransitive. *Intransitive* verbs do not take a direct object. (Transitive verbs are followed by a direct object.) Examples of *intransitive* verbs are 'come', 'arrive', 'dive', 'happen'. Such verbs can only be followed by an indirect object – to arrive at a place, to dive into the pool – or no object at all (one can't 'come' or 'happen' anything).

Some verbs can be transitive or intransitive according to the way they are used: e.g. 'steal', 'drop', 'climb', 'choose'. 'To steal a diamond' is a transitive use; 'to steal round the corner' is intransitive.

MAIN CLAUSE

A *main clause* is a group of words, containing a finite verb, which provides a coherent and complete statement in itself. The *main clause* (sometimes called an *independent clause*) is the linchpin of a sentence, and can make up a sentence by itself, without support from any additional material (examples from the <u>Independent on Sunday</u>):

"Scratch cards have all the characteristics of hard gambling."

Designer training shoes, for instance, are one of the consumer industry's most successful inventions.

(Each of these sentences has only one main clause, and no subordinate clauses.)

Sentences can be composed of two or more *main clauses*, linked by **and** or **but**:

Caley, aged 13, claims he doesn't care what he wears but in the same breath will admit to flouting school dress codes occasionally and wearing boots.

(there are two main clauses here and two main verbs: **claims** and **will admit**).

⇨ (See also SUBORDINATE CLAUSE in *Glossary*)

METAPHOR

A *metaphor* is a figure of speech, a word or phrase in which the language is used not literally, but so as to draw parallels between what is being described and something else. The difference between a literal use of language and a metaphorical one is illustrated by:

That's put the cat among the pigeons!

(None of the principal words is being used literally. Taken as a whole, the phrase means 'Now, that's really started some trouble!' The sentence is an extended metaphor, comparing a surprising and provocative situation with a real-life parallel indicated in the next sentence.)

The cat leapt from the windowsill and landed among the pigeons.

(Here the sentence means exactly what the words convey on the surface: a cat landed among some pigeons.)

It is impossible to think, write or speak without using language in a metaphorical way. Metaphors fill the air (itself a metaphor). Almost any excerpt from speech or writing will contain abundant metaphor – as this section of a newspaper paragraph shows (metaphors underlined):

Let the <u>cut-price bandwagon roll</u>, however, and the only people to benefit will be the <u>handful</u> who can <u>push their way</u> through the <u>real social barriers</u>, the perceptions of elitism and the patronising missionaries. We can carry on with an <u>overlay</u> of "high" cultivation... or we can choose instead to <u>feed the growth of an organic British culture</u> which <u>draws on</u> the diverse creative talents of all its people.

(Independent)

⇨ (See PERSONIFICATION, SIMILE in *Glossary*; CLICHÉ, LITERAL and MIXED METAPHORS in main section)

NOUN *(Part of speech)*

A noun is a name – of a person, a place, an object, a feeling, an idea. The first things we ever say are likely to be nouns (mama, car, dog), and they'll most probably be among our last words too.

Nouns fall into several categories:

Concrete nouns refer to <u>things which have a physical, measurable existence</u>:

pavement

arm

chestnut

trout

Abstract nouns describe <u>emotions, states of mind, qualities</u>:

fear

love

grief

trust

hope

expectation

Collective nouns refer to <u>groups</u> or <u>bodies</u> (of people, animals, etc.):

government

herd

crowd

audience

flock

orchestra

(It's not always clear whether a singular or plural verb form should be used with a collective noun. See NOUN / VERB AGREEMENT under NOUN in main section for further discussion.)

Proper nouns include <u>brand-names, our own names, the names of countries, towns, rivers</u>:

Coca-Cola

Swindon

Robert

Friday

February

France

Amazon

Wagner

(Proper nouns always take a capital letter, as do the adjectives derived from them [**French**; **Amazonian**; **Wagnerian**]. *See* CAPITAL LETTERS in main section.)

Compound nouns are made up of <u>two or more 'units'</u> and hyphenated:

ice-cap

change-over

slave-owner

cul-de-sac

go-slow

The hyphen should be used whether the compound is a familiar one, as above, or is an expression coined by the writer:

eco-villains

the policeman-turned-prosecutor

a concert-cum-rally

(Leaving out the hyphen can cause ambiguity; *see* HYPHEN in main section for further discussion)

OBJECT

The *object* of a clause or a sentence is the word or words which are in some way acted on by the verb. A *direct object* is immediately affected by the verb:

I saw <u>them</u> crossing the road.

An *indirect object* is not the immediate 'target', as it were, of the verb but is still involved in the action.

She delivered a powerful speech to <u>the audience</u>.

(*a powerful speech* is the direct object here; *the audience* is the indirect.)

⇨ (See also SUBJECT in *Glossary*)

ONOMATOPOEIA

Onomatopoeia is the creation of words in imitation of the sounds they indicate: fizz, gurgle, hiss, mew (or miaow), whinny.

Some writers, particularly poets, while not using words that are individually *onomatopoeic*, will select combinations of words that through accumulated sound produce an *onomatopoeic* effect. Here, the almost complete silence of a snowfall:

The only other sound's the sweep

Of easy wind and downy flake.

(Robert Frost)

OXYMORON

An *oxymoron* is a concentrated paradox, expressing in a couple of words something which looks on the surface to be contradictory but which experience shows to be true. When Juliet says to Romeo, 'Parting is such sweet sorrow', the last two words make an *oxymoron*.

⇨ (See PARADOX below)

PARADOX

A *paradox* is an idea or statement that, on the surface, seems to contradict itself but which, when examined, proves to have some truth in it:

There is a sense in which the sea is a desert, so that a man on a raft in mid-ocean is as surely doomed as a man in mid-Sahara, but it's a subtle desert, a sparkling desert ...

(Adam Mars-Jones, Independent)

"Just because you're clever doesn't mean you're not a blithering idiot."

(quoted in the Independent)

Paradox shouldn't be used to describe a straightforward contradiction where the ideas or facts simply don't square with each other.

⇨ (See OXYMORON above)

PARAGRAPH

The next unit up from the sentence, the *paragraph* is the most loosely defined of any grammatical terms. A *paragraph* must contain a single sentence but it need contain nothing more. Equally, a *paragraph* could run to dozens of sentences. A *paragraph* can be seen as dealing with a single aspect of a topic. It should have a unity of interest to it.

Changing *paragraphs* marks a change of direction, even if a slight one.

⇨ (See PARAGRAPH in main section)

PARENTHESIS *(Punctuation)*

Parenthesis is the term given to a comment in writing which is contained within brackets. Use of brackets, or *parentheses*, is generally reserved for additional (and non-vital) information, an author's own passing remark, etc:

... for one of her exclusive (and not cheap) lunch or dinner parties.

(The Times)

⇨ (See BRACKETS in main section)

PARTICIPLES

All verbs have participle forms. The *present participle* is invariably formed by adding *-ing*:

believing, climbing, hoping.

The majority of verbs form the *past participle* by adding *-ed*:

believed, climbed, hoped.

A number of verbs, some of them among the most frequently used, have irregular *past participle* forms: eaten, made, done, gone, begun, grown.

⇨ (See also UNATTACHED PARTICIPLES AND DANGLERS and VERB in main section)

PARTS OF SPEECH

There are eight parts of speech: noun, pronoun, adjective, verb, adverb, conjunction, preposition, interjection (or exclamation). Some linguistic experts would also include other classes of word under separate headings as parts of speech: prefixes; suffixes; and so-called determiners (words such as 'this' or 'that', and the definite and indefinite articles: the, a / an).

PASSIVE CONSTRUCTION

A sentence with a passive construction is one in which the word that would be the subject in an active construction becomes the recipient of the action of the verb. **The room was painted by me** is the passive formulation of the active construction **I painted the room**.

In the following,*are being burned* and *will be sent* are in the passive form while *believe* and *say* are in the active:

Kneecaps stolen from tombs are being burned as incense by burglars who believe victims will be sent to sleep, say police in the Philippines.

(Sun)

⇨ (See also ACTIVE CONSTRUCTION in *Glossary*, and VERB in main section for discussion of stylistic differences between active and passive.)

PERSONIFICATION

Personification is an example of the metaphorical use of language. It is the giving of human qualities to something which is inanimate: The cruel sea; the kind old sun; the treacherous mountain. *Personification* emerges in plenty of ordinary expressions like "It's been trying to rain all day" or "The weather was very good to us", where human attributes (of making an effort or of kindness) are transferred to something without any feeling at all. *Personification* can also be used in the sense of an embodiment, and is applied to someone who represents in a concentrated form some particular quality:

[Michael Milken] **a personification of the 1980s 'greed is good' mentality ...**

(The Times)

PHRASE

There is some debate among grammarians and language experts about the distinctions between *phrases* and *clauses*, and what follows is a tentative definition. A *phrase* is a set of words, even as few as one or two, which 'work together':

the black hat

taken by surprise

dead funny

    in the fuel tank

    turning right

    upside down

    London town

    steak and kidney pie

The following sentence:

    Motoring organisations welcome the move to tighten up on provisional drivers.

    (Daily Star)

could be broken up into a number of *phrases*:

Motoring organisations / welcome the move (it would be possible to further divide this as **welcome / the move**) **/ to tighten up on / provisional drivers.** The units that constitute a phrase ought to make a kind of sense together. For instance, if you took the consecutive words <u>**up on provisional**</u> from the sentence above you wouldn't have anything that was recognisably a *phrase* because the words do not stand effectively as a group.

Another way of identifying a *phrase* is by the absence of a finite verb in it.

    ⇨ (See VERB in *Glossary* for further description.)

PREFIX

Prefix is a verb meaning <u>to put in front of</u> or, as a noun, describes the combination of letters which are fixed on the front of words to change or refine their meaning.

Prefixes make negatives out of postives: un- (untidy); non- (nonsense); a- (asexual); im- (impossible); in- (indecisive).

They indicate frequency and number: re-order; retell; mono- (monorail); bi- (bilingual); tri- (triangle); quad- (quadruped), etc.

Prefixes indicate period / time / place: ante-chamber; post-war; pre-arrange.

They can also indicate attitude: pro-marketeer; anti-war.

    ⇨ (See also SUFFIX in *Glossary*, and HYPHEN in main section)

PREPOSITION *(Part of speech)*

Prepositions describe the relationship – the state of play – between the different parts of a sentence, and include such words as **under, in, through, with, behind, above.** Prepositions connect verbs and nouns, pronouns and nouns, etc. That archetypal sentence **The cat sat on the mat** hinges on the preposition 'on'. But the cat might also have sat **by, behind, near, opposite** the mat, and still been connected to it by a preposition.

    ⇨ (For problems associated with PREPOSITIONS see main section.)

PRONOUN *(Part of speech)*

Pronouns are substitutes for nouns and fall into various categories, among them:

personal: **I / you / he / she**

relative: **who / which**

demonstrative: **that / there**

reflexive: **myself / herself**

Some of the problems and confusions thrown up by pronoun use are dealt with in the main section: See BETWEEN YOU AND I; (PRONOUN AND) GENDER; WHICH / THAT;WHO / WHOM; WHO'S / WHOSE

PROSE

Prose describes almost all daily uses of language – in speech, in newpapers, TV and radio; in advertising and novels. Part of the dictionary definition is 'all writings not in verse', and although it is hard to distinguish exactly between poetry and *prose* by means of a definition, it is usually not to hard to recognise which is which in practice.

The adjective *prosaic* means matter-of-fact (as most prose is) and therefore carries the overtone dull.

PUN

A *pun* is a play on words which are similar in sound, or on words with a double meaning. Headline writers in some newspapers are remorseless punners:

Matt's Move Is Boot-iful

Vicar Cleared Of Flashing Has To Lock Up His Organ

(both Sun)

PUNCTUATION

Punctuation is the set of signs or symbols which, in written English, indicate pauses in the sense of what is being said.

Short pauses are marked by commas, long ones by full stops, or by colons and semi-colons. Dashes and brackets are ways of packing sentences more densely with information. Intonation (the rising of the voice) is indicated by a question mark; emphasis by an exclamation mark.

Punctuation, though seen by some as a minefield or a trap, is no more than a means of making meaning clearer, and is an essential part of written language where more than two or three words are gathered together.

QUESTION MARK *(Punctuation)*

The *question mark* signifies a direct question in speech or writing:

"How many tickets did you want?"

What did he do... ring the cones hotline?

(Sun)

Used in the middle of a sentence, and surrounded by brackets (?), the *question mark* is a standard way of expressing a writer's bafflement or uncertainty over something.

⇨ (See QUESTION MARK in main section)

QUOTATION MARKS *(Punctuation)*

Quotation marks (or speech marks) can appear singly (' ') or in pairs (" "). Their principal function is to denote direct speech:

"I hate the whole fashion thing," says Barbara.

(Big Issue)

but *quotation marks* have a variety of other uses, mostly to do with creating a distance between the writer and the words used:

The "book" is called _The Housekeeper's Diary_.

(the comment by Bernard Levin, in *The Times,* suggests that in his eyes it isn't a book at all)

⇨ (See QUOTATION MARKS in main section)

RELATIVE PRONOUN

Relative pronouns include 'who' and its variants ('whom', 'whose'), 'that' and 'which'. They occur at the start of subordinate clauses.

SEMI-COLON *(Punctuation)*

The semi-colon has been nicely defined by Godfrey Howard in _The Good English Guide_ as 'a heavy duty comma'. A full stop balanced on top of a comma, it marks a break in a sentence that is considerably stronger than the comma, and should be used when a writer does not want to separate two or more things into distinct sentences:

There is a soldier on the rebel side in the Liberian civil war; a schoolgirl in Cape Town ponders her career choices; tradition is represented by a nomadic chief in Mali.

(The Times)

As is the case with the use of the colon, the parts of a sentence separated by the semi-colon are closely related.

⇨ (See SEMI-COLON in main section)

SENTENCE

A *sentence* is a group of words, the first word of which begins with a capital and the last word of which is followed by a full stop or question or exclamation mark. It might also be defined as a group of words that will stand by themselves, making independent sense.

⇨ (See SENTENCE in main section)

SIMILE

A *simile*, a type of metaphor, is a comparison introduced by like or as. 'White as a sheet'; 'safe as houses'; 'move like greased lightning'; 'get on like a house on fire'. As the examples indicate similes tend to be well-worn, and many of them turn into clichés.

A good *simile* is likely to be one that is original and appropriate. Raymond Chandler, the creator of the 1940s private eye Philip Marlowe, was noted for the inventiveness of his *similes*. Some work; some don't.

... a wide path of freckles, like a mine-field on a war map.

... looking as unperturbed as a bank president refusing a loan.

She had eyes like strange sins.

⇨ (See METAPHOR and PERSONIFICATION in *Glossary*; CLICHÉ in main section)

STANDARD ENGLISH

Standard English is 'official' English. The quotation marks suggest the difficulty of defining exactly what that is. For general purposes standard English may be understood as the form of English that observes the rules and conventions laid down in dictionaries and grammar books. Standard English will also avoid the more marked examples of colloquial usage, and will avoid altogether slang and the local usages found in dialect or regional English. Standard English has sometimes been called BBC English, although there is a circular quality to this defintion (it's standard because the BBC uses it; the BBC uses it because it's standard). Nevertheless, there is some validity in the idea of a universal or standard style of language which, by avoidance of slang and dialect, and by adherence to a relative degree of formality and correctness, can be understood by everyone up and down the country. The kind of English used in national news broadcasting or in news reporting in most newspapers conforms to this sense of 'standard'.

SUBJECT

The *subject* of a clause or a sentence is the word or words that 'control' the verb. The subject can be:

a noun: **April is the cruellest month.**

a pronoun: **They walked rapidly across the road.**

or a phrase: **Cutting the lawn is a weekly chore.**

The *subject* usually goes before the verb, except when it forms part of a question (Is April the cruellest month?)

⇨ (See also Object in *Glossary*)

SUBORDINATE CLAUSE

A *subordinate clause* is a group of words usually containing a finite verb. *Subordinate clauses* don't make up complete sentences in themselves, because their meaning is tied to what is stated in the main clause. (Examples of subordinate clauses, underlined, from the *Independent on Sunday*.)

But although the urgency had gone, the curiosity remained.

If there was one place where he could still feel at home, it was the world of Scottish pantomime.

The first part of each sentence could not stand alone – that's what makes it a *subordinate clause*; the second part could – hence the term, *independent (or main) clause.*

A relative clause is one introduced by words such as **who, which, that**:

Already several people who have lost large amounts have contacted Gamblers Anonymous, the self-help group.

The relative clause here – **who have lost large amounts** – is dependent for its full sense on the *main clause* which surrounds it (**Already several people... have contacted Gamblers Anonymous...**) and, like an ordinary *subordinate clause*, it couldn't stand alone.

SUFFIX

A suffix is added to the end of a word to modify the meaning of that word:

-less: hopeless; fruitless; changeless

-ful: beautiful; suspenseful; powerful

⇨ (See also PREFIX in *Glossary*)

SUPERLATIVE *(ADJECTIVE)*

The superlative form of the adjective (used for a comparison of any number over two) is made by adding '-est' at the end of the adjective or by putting 'most' in front:

saddest

longest

most beautiful

most serious

⇨ (See also COMPARATIVE in *Glossary*)

SYNONYM

A *synonym* is a <u>word which has the same meaning as another word</u>.
'Open-handed', 'liberal', 'bountiful' are all synonyms for 'generous'.

English is rich in *synonyms* and *near-synonyms*, but a word rarely means
precisely the same as another word, and the right word in one context may be
subtly wrong (or less good) in another. Dictionaries are good at providing
synonyms – it's their job – but they don't give us the finer shades of meaning.
Only practice and exposure to language can do that.

(An *antonym* is the opposite to a *synonym*: ie, a word of opposite meaning to
another word [small / large; optimistic / pessimistic].)

SYNTAX

Syntax is the rules and conventions that indicate how sentences are put
together. For example, English *syntax* generally demands that adjectives go in
front of their nouns, or that objects follow the verbs that affect them.

TRANSITIVE VERB

A *transitive* verb takes a direct object:

> **Jackie, a former weightlifter who keeps her true identity a secret, has
> minded scores of stars, including Diana Ross and George Michael.**
>
> *(Daily Star)*

(*keeps* takes *identity* as a direct object; *minded* takes *scores*. Neither *keep* nor
mind could be used in the sense intended in this excerpt without being
followed by an object.)

An intransitive verb (such as 'come' or 'dive') can't take a direct object.

VERB *(Part of speech)*

The standard definition of *verb* is that it is a word indicating an action or a
state (a 'doing' word). Like the definitions of several parts of speech this isn't
particularly helpful, and it is rather easier to observe verbs in action in a
sentence than it is to say what they actually are.

> **I** think, **therefore I** am.

or

> **A girl student** was rescued **by firemen after she** spent **90 minutes with
> her hand** trapped **in a cola vending machine.**
>
> *(Sun)*

or

> **Tony** sighs **and** looks **down at his packet of cigarettes.** Being **an idol of
> the underaged** is **not always easy.**
>
> *(Time Out)*

Verbs are the motors of language. Without a finite verb a sentence is not, in strict terms, a sentence. *Finite* denotes any form of a verb that changes according to <u>person</u>:

I take *and* **he takes**

changes according to <u>number</u> (ie, between singular and plural):

she takes *and* **they take**

or changes according to <u>tense</u>:

they take *and* **you took**

The infinitive (**to take**), the present participle (**taking**) and the past participle (**taken**) are not finite forms, and therefore can't in themselves make up a complete sentence. For example, 'Take it' is a sentence (the 'you' at whom the command or request is directed being understood but not stated explicitly). But 'Taken it' or 'Taking it' are not sentences.

⇨ (see FULL STOP and SENTENCE entries in main section for fuller discussion).

INDEX

GLOSSARY CONTENTS

English Reference Books

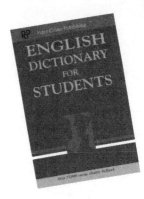

English Dictionary for Students
A comprehensive, up-to-date English
dictionary. With over 25,000 main entries;
each includes a clear definition, example
sentences, pronunciation guides, and
grammar notes.
ISBN 1-901659-06-2

English Thesaurus for Students
This reference book provides students with a
combined thesaurus and dictionary. Each entry
includes a definition and example sentences,
together with lists of synonyms and related
words. An ideal companion to the *English
Dictionary for Students.*
ISBN 1-901659-31-3

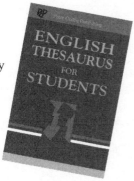

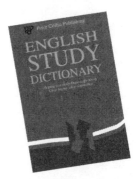

English Study Dictionary
A concise dictionary for learners of English.
Features a clear and easy-to-understand layout,
clear definitions of terms, example sentences,
pronunciation guides, and word-frequency
information to help with revision.
ISBN 1-901659-63-1

We publish a wide range of English and bilingual dictionaries,
workbooks and language reference material.

Peter Collin Publishing
32-34 Great Peter Street, London, SW1P 2DB
in the USA: c/o IPG, 814 N. Franklin Street, Chicago, IL 60610

www.petercollin.com